THE CUCKOO PAPERS

THE CUCKOO PAPERS

A Look at Misperceptions and Mistakes

JERRY BEAUCHAMP

authorHOUSE®

AuthorHouse™
1663 Liberty Drive
Bloomington, IN 47403
www.authorhouse.com
Phone: 1-800-839-8640

Published by AuthorHouse 07/02/2015

ISBN: 978-1-4772-8495-7 (sc)
ISBN: 978-1-4772-8494-0 (e)

Library of Congress Control Number: 2012922990

Print information available on the last page.

Dedication

This book is dedicated to my children: Sharon, Teri, Joe, Susie, and Mary Ann. As young children, they witnessed many mental cases and happenings during our time residing at the mental hospital. The hospital became a part of their early lives.

I also dedicate this to my loving wife, who lived every moment of this experience with me and who always supported my efforts to treat mentally ill patients. As a registered nurse, she was able to council me and the family during our eleven years at the San Antonio State Hospital. May God bless my wife, Clara Walker Beauchamp.

I must also give much credit to a fine dedicated doctor who, in my opinion, became the best superintendent the hospital ever experienced. A hospital of that type needs a Christian gentleman to oversee the treatments and care of the mentally ill. Dr. E. W. Bennett was that person.

Preface

In this book, I cover the early days of my adult life, which include almost eleven years of employment and schooling at an old mental hospital in San Antonio, Texas. There I met my beautiful wife while she was studying psychiatry as a student nurse. We married and later resided on the hospital campus. We were fortunate to birth five children as we lived on the employee campus, which was called SASH Village. Thus, my job at the hospital was a profession that involved my entire family.

Let me take you back to my beginnings prior to my work and study at this hospital.

Chapter 1

My Beginnings

I attended and graduated high school in the western part of Texas in the little town known of Ft. Stockton. The population was only about six thousand back in the late 1940s and into 1950 when I graduated from Ft. Stockton High School.

My father was an engineer for the Texas Highway Department. We lived in a very modest home in town. I remember the walls of our house were a foot thick. Located on Callahan Street, the home was an adobe building with plaster on the inside and outside. Central air was un-thought of in this era. However, it was fairly cool in the summer if we stayed inside; the thick walls protected the inside of the home from scorching west Texas heat. In the winter we turned on the natural gas space heater and the inside walls sometimes began to sweat. The home was probably more than seventy or eighty years old. Each adobe brick had been crafted by hand. I lived there more than sixty years ago and the modest Mexican built home is still standing. That would make it at least 150 years old as I write this book.

Back then Ft. Stockton was the hub of several road connections to towns like Alpine, Marathon, Sanderson, Monahan, and Great Falls. The area was very dry and hot during the summer days, but after sunset a cool breeze made the nights pleasant. I remember in early fall while traveling down Main Street I saw hundreds of tumbleweeds tumbling down the street past all the store fronts. The tumbleweeds were sometimes as big as washtubs.

On his way to work my father would drop my brother, sister and I at school. We lived about two miles from the school. As no school busses operated in our neighborhood, the other alternative was to walk, which we did many times. In the winter, after riding in the rumble seat of my father's 1936 Terraplane, my brother and I would arrive at school with our hair frozen stiff. It was still better than walking.

I graduated from Ft. Stockton High School in 1950. The next year my parents decided to move to San Antonio. My brother, Bud, stayed in Ft. Stockton and lived with the high school principal and his two sons. Bud was a good football player and, reluctant to lose his talent, the principal asked Bud to move in with his family. Bud lived with them until he graduated about two years later.

My father's position as a highway engineer gave me an opportunity to find summer employment with road contractors who knew him from our time in Pecos County, Texas. My father recommended me to a contractor, and I began working as a surveyor. I had learned a lot from my father about the road-building business. He taught me how to use and read the instruments and blueprints I used everyday in the highway surveyor job.

For three months one summer during school vacation, I was hired to work in the Big Bend National Park. Big Bend did not have paved roads then. Our job was to survey the desert and build a road down into the park from Marfa, Texas. Given that Big Bend was a National Park, we could not alter the environment in any way. This included killing living things, including rattlesnakes. If we saw a rattlesnake, we were told to turn and go around it. Preserving the environment also included replacing the desert stones we unearthed during constructions back on top of the ground.

Only the roadbed could be excavated. There could be no man-made ditches or even a water runoff trench next to the roadway. While I worked there it didn't rain much on site, but it did in the mountains. The runoff sometimes flooded the area and water covered the roads without any warning. Sometimes a stream of water a mile wide would suddenly appear. The water completely covered the road construction area. In an hour or two, we were in the middle of dry land again. This was strange indeed since there had been no visible rain clouds to warn us.

The scenery was a sight to behold. Great mountains with large trees were all around us. Trees were scarce in the desert near Ft. Stockton, so this was all new to me. It was extremely hot during the daylight hours, but at night I needed a light blanket while sleeping, even during the summer months.

On my first day I arrived at the end of a road in the vast park. An old Adobe ranch house stood ready to greet me. This old house was my living quarters for at least three months. The road contractor had hired a cook from some nearby ranch. The food was very good and plentiful. The cook served big breakfasts and packed all the road hands a sack lunch.

We returned to the house around 6:30 p.m. each day and enjoyed a big supper. There was a makeshift shower that we all made good use of. Water was provided from a windmill and earthen water tank. It took several minutes to wash off all the dust from the roadwork. Most of us showered before we ate, but some of the hands did not shower until after they had finished the supper meal.

There were a couple of radios for us to enjoy. The only drawback for me was that all the music and other programs were in Spanish. Big Bend Park was too remote to pick up American radio stations. When the radio was on it played a station from Mexico; Oneija, Mexico, I think. That was the only outside entertainment available. I recall advertisements on the radio from some doctor. He was always talking about "goat gland surgery" that would take care of a man's impotence. The surgery was performed just across the border in Mexico. Even though the radio programs were all in Spanish, aside from the doctor's advertisement, we enjoyed the music. It was just as well because we were all exhausted from the day's work at the hot, dusty construction sites.

The ranch house was built entirely with adobe bricks. The walls were almost a foot thick. It reminded me of our home in Ft. Stockton. I know the ranch house was at least a hundred years old at the time. The contractor furnished me with a retired army jeep to travel to and from the road site everyday. It also came in handy when traveling the new road to accomplish my surveying. Help was very scarce, as there were no homes close by and absolutely no cities.

This wasn't my first experience working a summer job with roadways. Previously, during my summer vacation from high school in Ft. Stockton, I'd had a part-time job with the Texas Highway Department. Every summer after school was out, I worked in the district office. One of my jobs was cleaning the blueprint film with carbon-tetrachloride. These drawings created the road elevation topography prints. The sheets were used again and again. I guess the film was some type of colloid, as plastics were not yet on the market. Carbon-tetrachloride had a very strong odor, and the fumes always got into my mouth and eyes. I sat under a ceiling fan, which seemed to help some, but the fumes were really bad. Once the films were cleaned, they were ready to reuse.

I also learned how to plot elevations, which became part of the blueprints used for the road contractors in the field. The work was done on the film and later the film was exposed to a blueprinting device. The printing device had to be prepared with ammonia fluid. The ammonia caused the prints to appear on a special type of paper.

Years later, after I was in the field and working on road jobs, I was told that carbon-tectrachloride had been taken off the market. It was originally manufactured for use in fire extinguishers. Even though it had been used as a cleaning fluid and in fire extinguishers, it could no longer be used for either because of federal regulations.

While still in high school, I was hired as an official flagman on the highway from Marathon to Sanderson, Texas. Boy was this a boring job. In the midst of the hottest surroundings one could imagine, no less. The hot asphalt on the road reflected the 102–106 degree heat during the day with very little breeze.

I stayed with this job and roomed at Sanderson, Texas all summer, sleeping in a warehouse owned by the Texas Highway Department. We were supplied cots upon which to sleep. After about a week of exposure to the hot sun, my lips became swollen and blistered. The big straw hat I wore was supposed to help, but it didn't seem to do much good. My lips became so swollen and cracked that I could not eat or drink without them burning.

There was a small-town doctor who had an office in back of a drugstore in Sanderson. I visited his office one afternoon to get my face and lips treated. He applied gentian violet to my lips and gave me a bottle for my own use. I looked like a clown with my purple lips. Every time I ate or drank anything, my lips left a smudge of purple on the cup or glass containers. I don't know how widely this treatment was used, but it cleared up my problem. At that time, no one had ever heard of or used any type of sunscreen. I guess sunscreen creams had not yet been invented.

Later on, after I graduated from high school, I was offered a job in southern Texas, just across from the Mexican border. This was my first real lengthy job. It was located in a little town known as Zapata, Texas. Zapata would soon be entirely underwater as it lay in the zone for the future Lake Falcon on the Rio Grande River. I always thought Zapata got its name from the shape of the lower part of Texas; the region resembled a shoe, and the Spanish name for shoe is *zapata*. It turns out the area was named for famed revolutionary, Jose Antonio de Zapata, after the war with Mexico.

The old town of Zapata was primarily composed of folks of Mexican descent. Most of the residents were ranch employees whose families had emigrated from Mexico, just a stone's throw from the small town.

Zapata needed to be relocated to higher ground. This operation created many new jobs. Some crews were required to pack up the homes while others were in charge of relocating families to their new town. The local cemetery and all the graves also had to be moved to the area that would be the new Zapata, two or three miles east of the original town. When I arrived, many families had already moved to the higher ground. Several old buildings and family dwellings had been abandoned, but were still standing. Some of the folks had to be forcibly moved. Most of the buildings and local housing were left intact, as the water would soon cover them all.

My employer had a contract to relocate the highway to higher ground. One of the abandoned buildings left in tact was the old Zapata hotel on Main Street. The firm that employed me had opened up the old hotel and provided beds for the guys working on the highway job site. This was my place of residence for the duration of my employment. The only businesses to speak of in Old Zapata were a few cafés, a gas filling station, an auto repair shop, and a small privately owned bank. There was also a little saddle and shoe shop that had to be moved.

The town's only bank had not yet relocated. It was called the Bank of Zapata. The bank's sign notified customers that the bank was "unincorporated" and "uninsured." I did not know exactly what that meant or how it might affect me. However, they were nice and set up a checking account for me with no trouble. The bank had been operated by a local Mexican family for at least sixty years.

Another Mexican family that continued to reside in old Zapata introduced me to one of the wives who did laundry. Each day, I left my dirty clothes in a pile in the hotel room. The Mexican lady picked them up, took them to the banks of the Rio Grande River, and washed them entirely by hand on the bank. She returned the clothes well washed, heavily starched, ironed, and ready for me to wear. As I remember, this cleaning cost only a few cents per item—a real bargain even in those days.

During workdays, I surveyed the roadway. The Texas Highway Department placed reference points about every two hundred feet at the new proposed highway site. I used these reference points to survey and placed grade stakes on the site of the new roadway. Those stakes indicated to the machine operators how much to excavate or fill for the base of the road.

I was allowed to hire two young Mexican men to assist me in the work. Both spoke almost no English and had probably never received formal schooling. I think they both lived on nearby ranches. One was married, and the other was single. They had never worked for a contractor nor done any type of work outside of ranching. They were very friendly and eager earn some extra funds for their families.

I instructed both men on how to read the measuring chain. They soon were able to measure the roadway. They also learned to locate the grade stakes with the help of my surveying ability. Our part had to be done before any road equipment came onto the site. This job lasted about a year. During that time, I realized that a hot and dusty job on the highway was not for me. However, I stayed on the job for the duration.

The pay was good and I saved almost all my salary. I purchased a nice late model vehicle, a 1949 Dodge Sedan, that replaced my worn out Kaiser sedan (probably a 1948 model). The Kaiser had an aluminum motor, and no one within a hundred miles knew how to repair it. I junked it in Zapata. The new Dodge was a shiny black color, and the inside was paneled with a wood-grain finish. It was my first "upgrade" vehicle. I was very proud of this car and took very good care of it. There was no air conditioner and the tinted window choice had not been perfected. Having never been in an air-conditioned vehicle, I didn't consider it a necessity. It did have a floor heater, which came in handy during the winter. June 1950 was indeed very hot; sometimes the temperature reached 102 degrees. Driving with the windows down was pleasant as long as the car was moving.

When my job on the highway was about to end, I notified the contractor that I would be leaving in about a week. I had saved what seemed like a lot of money while working in Zapata. Since I hadn't taken up drinking beer or smoking, there had been absolutely no place to spend money except on food and my laundry needs. I decided to take my savings and return to San Antonio to look for new opportunities.

A couple years after leaving, I revisited the Zapata site. I could see the tops of the old hotel and some of the other buildings in the middle of the lake. The water had almost covered all the structures. The view off the new highway is about as close as one could get to the old town.

There was a road that went down to the new dam if a person wanted to cross the river and enter Roma, Mexico. Roma folks had not been as lucky as residents on the American side when the lake was formed. The Mexican government had only told them to leave, whereas on the American side the government had constructed the residents' new homes high above the dam. Some of the Roma residents had slipped into Zapata from Mexico. There had been no sign of any law enforcement, so these immigrants had set up housekeeping in the new Zapata. There were no building restrictions except in the proposed flood area, so the immigrants seemed to be free to come, stay, build their homes, and find work.

Chapter 2

My Job Interview at the San Antonio State Hospital

After the job in Zapata, I moved back in with my parents in San Antonio. After about a week of relaxation at my parent's home, I felt it was time for me to find a career or go to school. At that time, the San Antonio State Hospital had been aggressively looking for new applicants. The "free education" plum was part of their new publicity efforts.

I inquired at the hospital and was given an appointment for my first interview. Driving my 1949 Dodge, I arrived at the San Antonio State Hospital for a job interview early on a Monday morning. Pulling up to the front gate of the San Antonio State Hospital for the mentally ill, my heart sank. This seemed to be the beginning of what would surely be a horrible experience. I had no idea what could be waiting for me behind all those locked doors.

Behind the main gate was a very large, old three-story building with a sign in front: *Administration Building*. I remember the tall wooden doors at the entrance. The doors must have been eight or nine feet tall. It reminded me of an old university building and campus I had seen in pictures. There were at least a dozen other buildings, most with three stories.

My appointment was at 8:00 a.m. I was to contact the personnel director, Mr. Lloyd. As I approached his office, I had a creepy feeling in my bones. Nevertheless, I proceeded to the office, which was located on the first floor of the huge building. Mr. Lloyd was very congenial and well mannered, but he appeared to be a highly persuasive individual. Mr. Lloyd told me I was well suited for a job in nursing services. They had recently initiated a new program of working and studying psychiatry while on the job.

I had a lot of reservations about joining the nursing services. I must admit that the offer sounded like a job for females and I had a feeling that this is no place for an "innocent" young boy. But I learned that my assignment would be for the male wards, as women operated the female wards. After much deliberation, I accepted the position.

After I was hired, I quickly enrolled in the work-education program provided by the Board for State Hospitals and Special Schools. The program seemed to satisfy my eager desire to work while studying. Having never been in a hospital setting, I still had my doubts about a nursing position, but I decided to hang around and see what the program had to offer. Back then my philosophy—for lack of a better term—was that I should try the system out for a while, even though the contract was for a twenty-four month commitment.

My Work-Study Commitment and Contract

Mr. Lloyd signed me up as an employee and told me to return the next morning at 8:00 a.m. At that time I would be introduced to the supervisors and directors of the hospital. My salary would be approximately $175.00 per month and included free schooling.

The work schedule would be 6:45 a.m. until 3:00 p.m. Monday through Friday. I was offered room and board for an extra $15.00 per month, but I chose not to reside at the hospital at that time. My gut feeling was that eight hours a day would probably be enough at the hospital. Also, living off the premises would provide a good time to rest and study, so I choose to continue living at home with my parents.

I did not sleep very well that Monday night, thinking maybe I had made a mistake about the entire program. I had never spent time with the mentally ill and had a preconceived idea that most of them would be mean and aggressive. The promise of a free college education was the only thing that got me back to the hospital the next day.

Early on Tuesday, I drove back to the hospital. I felt very uncomfortable wearing the new heavily starched white uniform. My uniform consisted of a white cotton shirt, white pants, white leather shoes and a black bow tie. I thought I stood out like a sore thumb. Once inside I became more comfortable, as all the employees and staff were dressed in the same type of uniform.

The Hospital Nursing Service

I met with Mrs. Ernestine, the director of nursing. She was an older lady, probably in her sixties, dressed in a heavily starched white uniform. She dressed as most nurses did in those days, complete with a starched white nurse's cap on her head that looked like a bonnet. She looked like an advertisement for Mrs. Clean. Her assistant, Mrs. Mary, was dressed in the same fashion except her cap was like the regular nursing caps of that era.

Both she and Mrs. Mary seemed happy to get a young man as one of their employees. I later found out most of the ward employees were old, and many had never finished grade school (with the exception of the newer hires). There were also a lot of husband-and-wife teams in the hospital's employ. The meeting was very brief, but Mrs. Ernestine made a point of asking me to make sure this was what I wanted to be doing. Over the first couple months, I would change my mind several times about this new career, but for the time being, I decided to hang on for the twenty-four month period.

The San Antonio State Hospital for the Mentally Ill

The San Antonio State Hospital (or SASH) as you see it today is a far different place than existed more than one hundred years ago. Yet some things never change.

In 1892, the Southwest Lunatic Asylum opened on the southern edge of San Antonio. Nestled among many pecan trees and situated on 640 acres, the pastoral setting, with its tree-lined main entrance on South Presa Street, offered asylum in the truest sense of the word. The asylum was a self-contained living environment for patients and staff. Crops and livestock were raised on the grounds, which at the time included all the land across South Presa Street and right up to the banks of the San Antonio River.

A large lake provided fishing and recreational activities for the patients. All resident staff members lived on the grounds, and even staff needed permission before leaving the hospital grounds for any reason. The hospital also included a cemetery where patients were buried when other family arrangements were not possible.

It was not until 1925 that the words *lunatic* and *asylum* were removed from the titles of mental institutions and replaced by a new name: state hospital. Nothing else was changed except the new name for the treatment center.

In the beginning, each mental hospital in the state was managed by its own individual board of managers, which reported directly to the governor of Texas. From 1920 to 1970, SASH became increasingly crowded. During these times as many as 3,000 patients were treated by only three hundred staff members. The facility was overcrowded by almost 1,500 patients. In contrast, in 2008 approximately 302 patients received treatment from a staff of 912. This alone provided a better treatment center. [1]

Due to this severe overcrowding, a great number of patients were transferred to other facilities, but some were simply released with no preparation or access to appropriate medical treatment or even counseling. Many of these released or discharged mental patients became homeless, and a great number slept under bridges and overpasses in the city.

In 1965, increasing research and awareness of mental health resulted in the Texas legislature passing the Texas Mental Health and Mental Retardation Act. This act established the Texas Department of Mental Health and Mental Retardation (TDMHMR). The new agency's purpose was to observe and restore the mental health of Texas citizens and to help people with mental retardation achieve their potential.

---

1 "San Antonio State Hospital," last modified on February 1, 2013, http://www.tshaonline.org/handbook/online/articles/sbs04

Chapter 3

Hospital Campus Layout

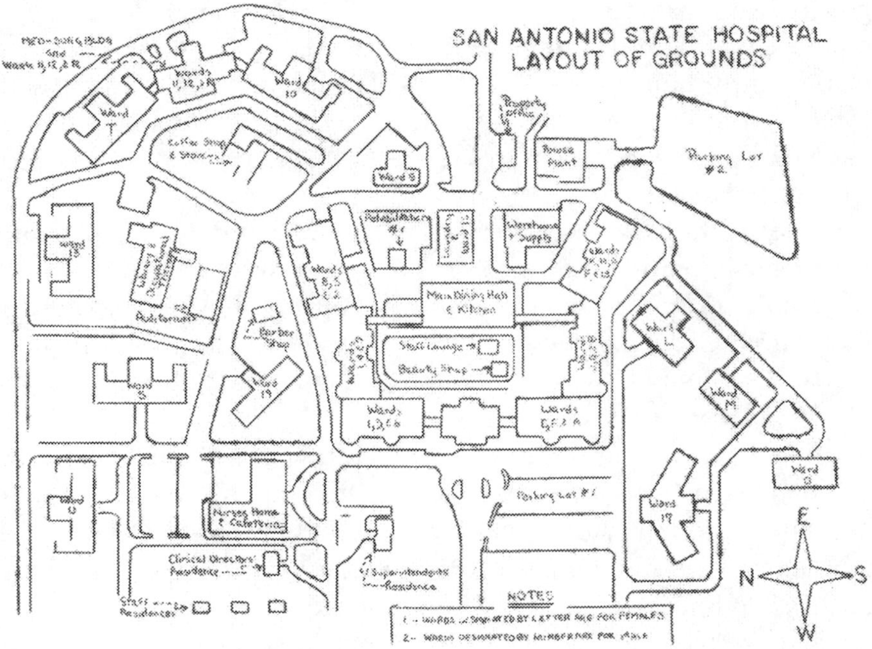

The 1950s San Antonio State Hospital campus layout

There were several large buildings on the hospital campus; most had three stories. Wire grates covered all the windows and enclosed the buildings' porches, where the patients stood and watched folks pass by.

Six of the buildings were used for patient housing. For the most part, the female patient wards were located on the south end of campus, while the male patient wards were on the north end. There were a few separate buildings throughout the campus also used to house patients. One such building was the hospital clinic. The clinic housed the seriously physically ill patients as well as the surgical operating room and the morgue.

Admissions

Entering the grounds of the hospital, the first large building was the Administration Building. It housed the offices of the superintendent, the clinical director, nursing services, personnel, and the medical file room. Adjoining the clinical director's office was the admissions office. The office was divided between a female supervisor for the female wards and a male supervisor for the male wards.

All new admissions were processed through either the male supervisor's office or the female supervisor's office. Usually a police officer or sheriff brought the mentally ill into the clinical director's office, and the clinical director would do a quick examination of the soon-to-be hospital patient. Upon arrival, every new admission was fingerprinted. Within two years, when the Polaroid camera became available, all patients were photographed upon admission too.

Depending on the first examination of the patient by the clinical director, they were assigned to a ward according to their diagnoses. The age and gender of the patient also determined which ward was chosen. The ward supervisor's phone would ring, and he or she was then instructed to come in and take custody of the new mental patient. The patient was then taken to the supervisor's office where the admission procedure began. Upon completion, the supervisor made a call to the respective ward, and an attendant would come and take the patient to his or her assigned ward.

The Surgery Ward

Patients were transferred to the surgery ward for all surgeries, including lobotomies. Since the hospital housed both male and female patients, there were occasional pregnancies. The surgical wing was used for labor and delivery for these patients. The babies were then placed for adoption through a local adoption agency.

The Nursing Service Department

The Nursing Service offices were also located on the first floor of the Administration Building. The male and female supervisors' offices were connected to the nursing service offices. Each supervisor oversaw all the attendants. Each ward had at least two attendants who operated it during the day. On evening and night shifts, there was only one attendant per ward. The only exception to that was the criminal ward, which usually had at least two attendants present at all times.

Patients over sixty-five usually went to the geriatric ward. Younger patients were admitted to other wards. Alcoholics were usually sent to the alcoholic ward.

After a while, I realized that some of the so-called alcoholics were sent to the hospital to escape pending legal charges. Usually these patients had charges of theft, swindling, robbery, or rape on their records. There was some appearance that a stay in the hospital would be an easy escape. The wealth of these individuals often determined whether or not they were eligible as alcoholics. The newer staff and nursing students saw through this procedure very quickly.

These supposedly alcoholic patients were treated very differently than other patients. They received a different food menu and different, if any, treatment. They even had more ground privileges. For them, it seemed to be a hotel atmosphere not usually found in a mental hospital.

There were some actual alcoholic patients, but they did not stay too long on the alcoholic ward. If their prognosis was low after treatment, they were transferred to the general wards. It depended on the risk involved with them. If the flight risk was low, they were transferred to a minimum security ward. This type of ward was usually unlocked during the day so patients had full benefit of the grounds and the little store.

The Chaplains

There was always a resident chaplain at the hospital, at least during the early 1950s. The chaplain was an important part of the patients' treatment and rehabilitation process. Patients were also ministered to by a Catholic priest who resided in the nearby Mission San Jose. However, the resident chaplain was the main one; working daily, counseling patients, and serving as the hospital volunteer council. In the late 1950s, a chapel was constructed by the hospital and funded mostly by the volunteer council.

Working with the volunteer council and the chaplain's office was a staff person named Bertha. She did all the running around and gathering of clothes donations for the patients. Bertha also made many trips with patients who had off-campus doctor appointments. I think she must have worked at the hospital for about forty years. She was indeed a patient's advocate. Bertha had a special report with the superintendent of the hospital, especially during the term of Dr. Bennett. Dr. Bennett relied on her for many chores that the regular staff was unable to perform. Bertha arranged and managed the annual hospital parade that was the highlight for most of the patients.

Sacraments at a Hospital Mass

One of the chaplains told me he used plain grape juice for the sacraments. On the other hand, a Catholic chaplain used real wine. He said his wine was always in short supply, and some went missing on several occasions. One day a note was placed in one of the chaplain's supply cabinets. The note had been written by a patient, who stated that he did not like the wine used by the other chaplain and helped himself to the Catholic chaplain's supply.

This was a joke among the chaplains. Thereafter, the wine had to be locked up so there would be some for the chaplain to use in his service. Even though they discovered who was taking the wine, no punishment was ever given to the patient.

The Criminal Ward

The criminal ward housed only male patients and required more staff, at least four or five attendants, during the 7:00 a.m. to 3:00 p.m. shift. The day shift was mainly responsible for giving treatments and supervising the more active patients. Many patients who had committed crimes, such as murder and aggravated rape, posed a direct threat to the other patients in the hospital and were considered a high escape risk. There were approximately 120 of these patients, many of whom were court committed to the hospital.

Chapter 4

My First Assignment

The next person to greet me on my first day was Mr. Howard, the supervisor of the male unit. Like me, he was dressed in a white starched uniform, complete with a black tie and white shoes. Attached to his black belt was the largest ring of keys I had ever seen. He smoked like a chimney, which annoyed me since I had never taken up smoking.

Mr. Howard briefly gave me orders and provided me with a set of large, jail-like skeleton keys. I was told that I should sign in each morning in his office and pick up the keys to my assigned ward. After 3:00 p.m., I was to return the keys to the large locked cabinet. I was never to take the keys off the premises.

With keys in hand, Mr. Howard and I began the walk to my assigned building. It was during that walk that Mr. Howard informed me I'd been assigned to Ward 12…the criminal ward. My heart sank. It was my first day, and I was going to the criminal ward. Had I made a mistake?

Ward 12 was located on the top floor of a three-story building on the male side of campus. We passed through several locked doors before finally arriving at the top floor.

Inside the Criminal Ward

Mr. Howard handed me over to Mr. Lee, my immediate supervisor. He was an older gentleman, probably in his sixties, who had a German or Polish accent.

Mr. Lee took me around the ward. It held 145 male patients, most of who had been committed to the hospital ten to twenty years ago. We toured the individual locked cells, where he pointed out several patients, specifically the combative ones. Mr. Lee explained that these patients were the worst of the lot. He cautioned me to be very careful when approaching them. Mr. Lee was careful to point out that many of them had cerebral spinal syphilis, which caused brain damage. Any contact with these patients was to be done with extreme caution.

Our next stop was a large dormitory with more cots than I had ever seen in one place. Mr. Lee said no patient was to enter this dorm unless he was going to mop and clean it. The dorm was for sleeping only.

Next was the clothing room. In this room were stacks of blue overall pants. There was a bin for socks and underwear and racks for work shoes. Another room housed towels, soap, and more undergarments. There seemed to be enough clothing in those two rooms to outfit a small army. Everything was the same style and design, even the work shoes. At one end of the storeroom there were stacks of blocked tobacco and boxes of chewing tobacco that resembled twisted rope. It looked like there was enough Bull Durham smoking tobacco to provide each patient a month's supply.

We then toured the bathroom and toilets. The bathroom was long and narrow with a wall of open shower stalls. About fifteen toilets stood opposite the shower stalls. The toilets were lined up in two rows. Everything was open. I was amazed at the cleanliness of each room.

Just outside of the main dorm was a large closed-in porch area. The porch was enclosed with chain-link type grating from top to bottom. There were many patients hanging on the fence, smoking and chewing tobacco.

I thought it strange that none of the patients were conversing with each other. They were just standing or sitting and staring into the courtyard three stories below. Later, I discovered that the patients in this setting never spoke with one another. Perhaps the mental illnesses they suffered from forced them to ignore their surroundings. Each patient's mind apparently didn't run on the same track as the other patients. Deep inside their beings one could sense the lonely worlds in which they resided.

At times staff members were able to converse with the patients on a one-on-one basis. While the trained attendants and nursing staff were able to ask simple questions and receive short answers, it seemed impossible to carry on a lengthy conversation with these patients. Chronic mental illness evidently controlled their thinking.

Thus, the patients lived within their own worlds and retreated into their own shells.

Many patients talked to themselves, some loudly, and a few cursed. The cursing was not directed toward any single individual; most just shouted while hanging on the grating. Hallucinations caused some patients to answer their own thoughts out loud. This disease resulted in delusions, somewhat like a bad dream. Patients could become terrified by these delusions and be combative as a result. Sometimes a patient perceived someone in the hallucination attempting to assault him. Caretakers had to recognize these episodes and attempt to redirect the patient's thinking as quickly as possible.

The porch was a busy place, as most of the 145 patients were out there. Patients walked back and forth. Some fast, some slow, some just strolling in circles. Despite all the movement, without conversation, the porch usually remained pretty quiet. There were the occasional outbursts; someone screaming out loud, another repeating curse words over and over, some just yelling to the wind.

On the porch I met the ward attendants, Mr. Scott, Mr. Thomas, and Mr. Click. Mr. Scott and Mr. Thomas were active duty U.S. Air Force personnel. I think Mr. Click was also, but he never remarked about his profession. All three were making extra spending money by working as attendants for the hospital. All of the new hospital attendants hired from the Air Force were single. These men were the only employees who had been formally educated in schools and graduated from high school, with the exception of the registered nurses, physicians, and the employees attending in-house psychiatric school.

The hospital provided the Air Force men jobs with hours that were compatible with their official Air Force duties, allowing them to come and go as their schedule permitted. Most worked during the day if they were allowed to work away from the Air Force Base. These enlisted men could sign in and out during the day or night, even if only for a few hours. This was an exception to the rules, as regular employees had strict hours on one of three shifts: 7:00 a.m. to 3:00 p.m., 3:00 p.m. to 11:00 p.m., and 11:00 p.m. to 7:00 a.m.

All the Ward 12 patients were able-bodied and looked to be in good physical condition. The patients had just returned from their breakfast and were going to start their regular duties cleaning the ward. They seemed to be constantly cleaning and scrubbing. Mr. Scott said, "We must keep these guys very busy. Most of them never go outside and must be kept busy as part of their treatment on the ward." Later I learned that the work also kept them busy so they would rest at night. Keeping them occupied during the day seemed to help them sleep. Most of these patients never touched the actual ground in any way and only a handful of them ever received visits from their families.

For the entire first day, I just observed the ward, the patients, and especially the work the attendants had to do to manage them. There were a lot of mops and buckets moving around. The ward was about half the size of a football field, housing two dormitories filled with cots for the men to sleep on. All patients, except those locked in individual cells, slept in the dormitories.

Along the halls were the grated cells that housed the patients who had to be kept separate due to fighting, escape potential, or punishment. However, I was informed that we were never to mention the term *punishment*, mainly because the system was called a hospital, and hospitals did not punish patients. "Do not punish the patients," was the general order, but I saw several patients punished for actions like fighting or disobeying orders from the attendants. Usually the "punishment" was extra ward work.

There were about eight to ten separate cells with only one individual incarcerated in each. One cell was vacant. I discovered it was left open in case a patient became violent and had to be locked up. All patients who resided in the individual cells had been prescribed separation by the ward physician; some for being combative, others for their own protection from other patients. Attendants could lock a patient up temporarily until the ward doctor signed the order. Although most of the patients in the cells were a danger to others, several of them would at least converse when spoken to.

One cell housed a male patient who looked to be in his twenties. He was completely nude. There was no bed or chairs in his cell, only a bucket in the corner in which to defecate and urinate. I was told that this patient was extremely combative and would attempt to bite others unprovoked. He never spoke a word to anyone, but he often made sounds like a caged animal.

On that first day, one of the attendants released a patient from his cell and told him to go to the porch and pick up a mop or broom and begin cleaning the floors. He immediately left for the porch and did as he was told, completely ignoring the other patients.

Mr. Scott told me that tomorrow was "shock day." This meant a list of patients requiring shock therapy was presented to the ward doctor as he made his rounds. The doctor then made the final decision on who would or would not be shocked. Usually the doctor relied on the attendants to provide the shock list. The attendants knew the patients well, whereas the doctor only saw most of them once every several days and then just briefly. The attendants had already drafted a list for the next day.

The time now was 11:00 a.m., and all patients were told to line up to be counted. Everyone's name was called out to make sure they were in line for the noon meal. Everyone, that is, except those in separate cells; lunch would be delivered to them after the other patients returned to the ward. Roll calls were done at least four times per day to make sure all the patients assigned to Ward 12 were accounted for and in their proper places. Patients were counted before meals and also upon their return to the ward.

The three attendants and I were to escort the patients to the dining hall. Mr. Lee remained at the ward, as there were about four or five patients who did not march to the dining hall. Most of those who remained were in the locked cells. The charge attendant did not like to remain alone with the patients unless they were locked up.

Getting the patients in line for lunch was not much problem. They all knew to march down to the second floor and across an enclosed walkway to the adjoining building where the dining hall was located. In the dining hall, three meals were served each day on a regular schedule. Meals were all wholesome and freshly cooked by the dining room staff and patients. The dining hall was the largest dining facility I had ever seen. There were two separate serving lines, one for male patients and one for female patients. The dining hall's windows and doors were all made of grating.

It contained almost 1,000–1,200 male patients, all separated by their respective wards. On the opposite end of the dining hall, there were at least 1,000–1,500 female patients that dined at the same time. With a few thousand patients in one large room, the noise was so overwhelming that people had to yell to be heard. Separating the men's side from the women's was an island of kitchen equipment. Sometimes a patient would make a break for the other side of the room to visit members of the opposite sex. The same patients usually attempted this every time and they were often intercepted before reaching their destination.

Only residents of wards connected to the dining hall via enclosed walkways were able to eat in the large dining hall. Separate ramps served the male and female patients. The patients could move in and out of the dining hall and never set foot on the ground below.

Patients residing in other buildings ate and slept in their respective buildings. Usually the geriatric patients or the alcoholic patients resided on separate wards that had their own kitchens and dining room facilities.

Ward 12 was first in line to enter the dining hall. The operation was similar to cafeteria-style serving, but without choices in food. All patients received the same meal. Patients assigned to dining hall duty served the food. Once through the chow line, with divided metal tray of food in hand, the men were marched to Ward 12's usual picnic type table in the dining hall. The tables were made of heavy metal; they had shiny tops and were about twenty feet in length. The seats were attached to the tables.

Once seated, the attendants passed out large spoons for them to use as eating utensils. I was told that knives and forks could be used as weapons. Therefore, patients were only given spoons, which were counted again at the end of each meal to be sure none were taken back to the wards. Each patient was also issued a metal cup with a handle into which the attendants served fresh sweet milk, or buttermilk. Each attendant carried two large aluminum pitchers full of milk and served it to patients seated at the dining table.

The food was plentiful and wholesome, but not very appetizing compared to the food I was accustomed to eating. Each tray contained a large portion of meat, vegetables, and a dessert, usually a slice of cake. The patients usually ate every last bit of food on their trays. They usually were not served seconds; however, they could have another cup of milk if they desired. The servings were adequate for any normal meal. Some patients gulped their food down and would then attempt to steal food from other patients' trays. This usually caused fighting. Fighting in the dining room occurred almost daily.

Patients performed all the chores in the dining hall and were supervised by hospital employees. Both dining areas used patient labor to cart food from the dumbwaiter and serve it. These patients also did the cleanup in the dining areas, including washing all utensils. The kitchen on the first floor also used patients to help prepare and cart the food upstairs to the dining hall. All the cooked food was placed into the dumbwaiter for delivery to the dining area, which was on the floor above the food preparation room.

My Assignment in Surgery

Part of my psychiatric technician training required me to spend at least two weeks in the operating room. The room looked like any other operating room, and all the requisite sanitary requirements and protection was standard. Most of the surgical operations conducted involved the appendix, gall bladder, broken limbs, and delivery of babies.

I learned later that prefrontal lobotomies were performed in the operation room. If a patient required surgery for an illness or serious accident, surgeons from the city were contracted to perform the surgery.

Inventory Revealed Missing Drugs

One day I was assigned to clean the narcotic cabinet and inventory the contents. I discovered that several sodium pentothal vials were missing from the carton in the cabinet. After I called this to the attention of the in-charge operating room nurse, the result of the inventory was reported to the hospital superintendent. He began an investigation that found that a nurse who worked night duty had keys to the surgery unit. She also had possession of the keys to the cabinet. I was told that a search of her room at the nurse's dormitory had revealed that she had hidden several vials of the drug in her room. She was relieved of her duties and quietly left the hospital. I don't think she was ever convicted, and it was never reported to law enforcement as far as I know.

Autopsy Performed Adjacent to the Operating Room Theater

Another phase of my schooling was participation in autopsies. The morgue was attended by a staff physician with pathology experience. He was an older gentleman who had some type of palsy. He was very efficient in his work, and he enjoyed explaining to the students the entire process of the autopsy. Because of his thoroughness, my experience in the morgue was a great teaching phase of my study at the hospital. Students could visit the morgue at any time, but at some point during their schooling, all were required to assist in an autopsy.

Every patient who died in the hospital had an autopsy performed on them. As best I could determine, about two or three patients expired every week, so the morgue was a busy place all during my stay in that section of the hospital. Mostly, the doctor was interested in the makeup of the patients' brains. Jars containing brain lobes for further study lined the shelves in the autopsy room. It was a creepy sight to look around and see all the bottles of brains and tissues. I worked for about two weeks assisting the doctor with autopsies. I rotated between the operation room and the autopsy room during this phase of study.

I cannot forget the first autopsy where I assisted Dr. A. After he opened the abdomen and we began to remove organs, the doctor asked me to place a kidney on the table for observation. When the doctor cut into the kidney, a squirt of urine immediately hit my face and mouth. (I must point out there were no safeguards in place, not even a mask or goggles. We did, however, wear surgical gloves and a smock to protect our uniforms). Before the next autopsy, I borrowed masks, gloves, and surgical gowns from the surgery facility, making me feel somewhat more protected.

The medical staff was most interested in examining the brains. I suppose a mental patient's brain might somehow offer some understanding of the patient's mental illness. The doctor always dissected and examined the brain. The remains of the brain were usually placed in formaldehyde and kept on a shelf nearby.

After the required autopsy, most bodies were then buried in the hospital cemetery. Patient's families could claim the remains and have a private burial, but I never saw that happen. Most families did not even attend the services at the hospital cemetery. There was always a chaplain or priest in attendance but no other visitors.

Chapter 5

The Carpenter Shop

The hospital also maintained a carpenter shop; mainly to repair broken doors, windows and the ward grates. It also made keys for use at the hospital. The carpenter shop employees were all staff members of the hospital. Several patients were also assigned to assist the carpenters. The patients usually carried the tools and supplies.

Grates and doors were the big items constantly in need of repair. The grates were all very old and had to be repaired frequently. Some patients urinated on the porch and onto the grates, causing the metal to rust. The three-story buildings that housed long-term patients had to be repaired often. Usually the attendants of the respective wards did daily inspections of the grates, and if a grate needed repairing, an attendant would send a work order to the carpenter shop.

The Hospital Farm

The farm covered at least fifty acres in the river bottom of the San Antonio River. It was within walking distance of the hospital and therefore easily accessed by the patients. It grew mostly corn as well as other vegetables. The farm provided all the vegetables for the hospital. Patients did all the work and were supervised by the employee farm manager. The manager and his family lived in a home just across the street from the hospital, on the banks of the San Antonio River.

The usual farm equipment was housed there along with several wagons that hauled patients to and from the work areas. The wagons, pulled by tractors, could hold more than twenty patients, all dressed in blue overalls and straw hats, riding to a work destination. I was told that twenty years prior, draft horses had been used to pull the plows and wagons. This changed sometime in the late '40s or early '50s when the hospital purchased tractors. Daily there must have been around fifty patients working the farm.

A hog farm was also located on the grounds to supply meat for the patients. Wooden fences enclosed what must have been at least a hundred hogs. The hogs were well fed with scraps of food from the dining room. They were butchered in the food preparation room, where they were killed, skinned, and stored in refrigerated vaults.

During and prior to the '50s, all the milk served at the hospital was produced on premises. Patients milked the cows and the milk was transported by a wagon to the creamery for processing. At the creamery, buttermilk and butter were also produced. When the milk soured, it was placed in a large vat to make buttermilk. Chipped slices of fresh butter were placed into the buttermilk vat. The butter melted while the buttermilk was prepared. The buttermilk was then cooled in the vat, and the butter rose to the top. Then the buttermilk was churned so the butter would flake off and mix with the buttermilk. At one end of the creamery was an ice cream plant that supplied ice cream on certain days. I suppose the ice cream was prepared just like it would have been done in a commercial creamery. The ice cream was delicious; the rum raisin flavor was my favorite.

In the early '60s, the hospital system closed the farm and creamery. The hospital then purchased food from suppliers within the state. Vegetables and meat were also purchased from an outside supplier, as the cattle and hogs were also removed.

After the farm closed, the patients who worked there were reassigned to other areas of the hospital. Many of the patients who had worked at the farm had done so for more than forty or fifty years. They were relocated to various wards, where many became custodians. The patients weren't paid a salary. They worked full days and were given Sundays off.

The Hospital Fire Department—A Gruesome Discovery

Employees who resided on the hospital campus were encouraged to work in the fire department in addition to their regular duties. They were given discounts on their housing if they joined. Each month, the members rode the fire truck and checked out the fireplugs to make sure they had water available. Practice sessions were performed routinely.

One evening several months later, after I had moved onto the campus and joined the fire department, during one of our inspections we passed the carpenter shop. We could hear one of the table saws running even though the shop was closed. Upon further investigation, we found that a patient who usually worked in the shop had turned on the table saw, climbed up on the table, and placed his neck against the running saw blade. It had completely severed his head from his body. His head was still on the table, and his body was on the floor. Blood was everywhere.

According to law, we had to call the coroner in to make an investigation. One of the men stayed with the body until the coroner arrived. The patient was taken to the morgue and later autopsied and buried in the hospital cemetery. The cause of death was determined to be self-inflicted, and the ruling cleared the hospital of any wrongful charges. Evidently, the patient hid in a closet until all the employees had left for the day. He was usually on the cleanup detail at the carpenter shop. The medical staff determined the patient had planned the entire suicide alone.

The Hospital Shoe Shop

A shoe shop was also located on the hospital grounds to repair patients' shoes. There was one employee in the shop and several trustworthy patients doing the repairs and polishing the leather shoes. It was a big operation, since there were more than three thousand patients. Only the cell patients did not wear shoes. I noticed that the patients working in the shop also manufactured the shoestrings. There was a large round container of continuous string strap material they cut to length and fashioned into shoestrings.

The shoes, I was told, were manufactured at the state prisons and delivered to the various hospitals in the state. The blue overalls worn by the working patients were also manufactured in state prisons.

The Hospital Laundry

The laundry was responsible for cleaning the patients' clothes and bedding. All the employees had their uniforms cleaned, starched, and ironed in this facility as well. Employees had to purchase their own uniforms, but the cleaning was free. Mainly employees did the cleaning and ironing of uniforms.

Employees marked their names in each garment by hand with special black ink. Patients' garments were tagged by ward number. If a family chose to supply a patient's clothes, the clothes were sent to a marking room where the patient's full name and ward number were imprinted onto the garments by machine.

Sheets were laundered in large washing machines. Once clean, they were quickly placed in a drying and ironing machine. There was a continuous line of sheets going in and coming out to be folded and sent back to the wards. Bedding was usually replaced once per week unless it became soiled. The wards stored extra linens so replacement could be done without much delay.

The laundry facility was the second largest operation in the hospital. Food preparation and the dining hall were the largest of all and completely took up a large two-story building. Adjacent to the laundry facility was a sewing room, which repaired clothing and bed materials. Employees usually did the sewing and made repairs to these items.

The Hospital Pharmacy

Sometimes my duties included picking up supplies from the pharmacy. To illustrate a typical pharmacy run: One day Mr. Lee asked Mr. Scott and me to take four trusted patients with us to pick up medicine and supplies for the ward. At the pharmacy, we were issued bandages and first-aid supplies. There were also bottles of different types of medicine. Mostly the medications consisted of a pain reliever known then as APC. APC tablets were similar to what we know as Excedrin or a similar pain reliever.

We then went to the warehouse and picked up chewing tobacco, Bull Durham smoking tobacco, bathroom supplies, cleaning supplies, and a few new items of clothing that would be issued later. All male patients were issued a pair of blue overalls, the type most farmers wore during those years. Some tidy patients were allowed to receive private clothing. Families were encouraged to supply their relatives with clothing, but not many did beyond when a patient was first admitted.

Loaded down with supplies, we returned to the ward. The patients knew exactly where everything belonged and began to sort and store the supplies. The medicines were taken directly to the ward office. All were counted and locked in the medicine cabinet.

Typically, the only medicines stored on site were common, such as APC for headaches and castor oil for constipation. Some alcohol was issued to the wards for emergency wound cleaning. The alcohol was prepared in the pharmacy, where it was colored green to distinguish it as a medical item. No sleeping pills or antibiotics were kept in the medicine cabinet. However, antibiotics were available in the clinic. Penicillin was the drug of choice, and was administered by a nurse in the clinic. Not many other medications were prescribed, as tranquilizers were not yet commonly used. It appeared that shock treatments were the only methods of controlling the patients' outbursts and depression.

The Hospital Tunnels

There were tunnels directly under the old ward buildings. They originally housed the first mentally ill patients back in the 1800s. Originally, the tunnels had a sort of rail track that had enabled supplies and food to be delivered to the cells. The steel doors and steel bars erected in the 1800s were still in place in the tunnels. Some of the old tunnel cells were also converted into storage rooms for discarded hospital equipment and old files. The tunnels were all closed off during the early 1940s.

The Liquor Stash

The tunnels also housed a closed room with a steel door that contained many boxes of liquor. I was told the liquor had been confiscated during the prohibition era in the 1920s and given to the hospital to be used as sedatives for the patients. This area was filled with boxes of unopened whiskey, wine, and other spirits.

Rumors were that the staff doctors regularly used the liquor for their own use. The hospital pharmacist held the key to the liquor room. It was strictly off limits to all employees.

However, I did hear that a group of part-time air force enlisted men had heard about the liquor, and one night several of them busted the steel door open and retrieved several boxes of liquor. No one caught them, so they took what they could, and nothing was ever publicly mentioned.

Chapter 6

Forms of Mental Health Treatment during the Early 1950s through the 1960s

During my tenure at the San Antonio State Hospital, in the early 1950s and into the 1960s, the following methods were used for treating mental health issues:

- Patients locked in wards, some in cells
- Electroshock treatment
- Insulin shock treatment
- Prefrontal lobotomies
- Selective hydrotherapy (abandoned in the early 1950s)
- Occupational therapy
- Industrial therapy
- Sheltered workshop (began in the mid-1960s)
- Counseling (mainly for alcoholic patients)
- Church services
- Recreation therapy (usually weekly hospital dances)
- Industrial therapy (extremely new for the mental hospitals in 1953)

In addition to the list above, in the late 1950s or early 1960s, tranquilizers became the best method of treating mentally ill patients. Daily work schedules, such as the laundry, farm, kitchen, and janitorial were performed under the direction of the Industrial Therapy Department. Patients were also given free time at La Tienda (the campus store for patients).

TB Treatments

Patients needing tuberculosis treatments were confined to the special TB ward. Several hundred patients contracted tuberculosis, either prior to or after admission. About half of the TB patients were male.

The tuberculosis treatments were highly successful. A physician who had transferred to the United States from Cuba took extreme interest in the disease and had great success with his treatments. During my schooling, I rotated through this ward and learned about the new treatments. My time there required extreme caution. Staff members were required to wear masks, gowns, and special shoe coverings. Regular hand washing was a must.

Many new drugs were available to treat TB, but it was the fluoroscope that allowed for major breakthroughs in treatment. A fluoroscope uses x-rays to provide real-time moving images of the inside of the body. The doctor using the fluoroscope could accurately inject medicine into the damaged area of the lung. The pressure of the medicine would cause the lung lobe to come together and squeeze out the tumor. This treatment was continued over several months until the TB lesion completely disappeared.

Patients were also given oral medications in the beginning of the treatment phase. This medication helped stabilize the lesion and reduce its size. The entire treatment time varied, but most patients began to recover from the disease in as soon as three to six months and almost always within a year.

Counseling of Patients

Newer patients received more direct treatment and counseling by doctors and therapists. For patients who had been hospitalized for many years, staff doctors conducted limited direct counseling. The seasoned patients, many of whom had been housed at the hospital for more than twenty years, mainly received maintenance drug therapy such as tranquilizers (when they became available for treatments) and other necessary medications. The work performed on wards and hospital grounds was the treatment for most of the seasoned patients. The majority of these patients had been completely forgotten by their families. It was very seldom that any of them received visitors.

The hospital chaplains also counseled patients and their work was in great demand. Only two hospital chaplains were available for three thousand patients. Patients were selected by the staff doctors and sent to the chaplain's office. Sometimes they had to wait weeks to see the overworked chaplains.

In actuality, the majority of patients received no actual treatment and were merely kept locked up all their lives. The main reason for this was that the older committed patients had outlived their illnesses or were not reachable with current treatments. These were the patients I classed as "castoffs." No relatives visited them and they were kept from the outside world for their own safety and the safety of others. Even if they had been eligible for discharge, many had no place to go.

If a patient outlived his or her mental illness and was judged to be safe around others, he or she was placed on an open ward. An open ward was kept unlocked during the day and closed at night. I guess these patients could be classified as trustworthy patients. They were allowed to come and go during the day. However, only a few were given an extra pass to leave the hospital grounds by strolling through the hospital gates. They later returned for the night. If they were fortunate to have a few dollars, they could catch the bus and travel to the city for a day outing.

It is important to note that since the 1960s, much has changed in the care and treatment of the mentally ill. I don't recall that upon discharge the hospital merely dropped a mental patient off at a bus station and gave him or her a ticket to get out of the city. I had almost finished writing this book when this kind of story appeared in my local newspaper.

The article reported that many of the patients who were eligible to go home were discharged from the hospital. Families were notified, but many of the patients were never picked up. The hospital provided them with bus tickets to their last known addresses. Some of these patients became homeless, and some set up house under bridges or places that were out of the way of other citizens.

The article ran in the *Express-News*, a local newspaper in San Antonio, on Friday, May 22, 2009[2]. It exposed this type of patient discharge, which is now being investigated by state authorities. The

---

2 Karisa King, "Patient Drop-Offs Targeted," *San Antonio Express-News*, May 22, 2009.

Express-News reported that a San Antonio State Hospital patient named Raquel Padilla, called Rachel by family members, was found dead three days after she was dropped off in downtown San Antonio. No one knew how Raquel Padilla died—not the medical examiner, not the police, and not her family members, who had entrusted her to the San Antonio State Hospital.

The *Express-News* further stated that the only thing clear about her final days was that Padilla, who was fifty-four and had schizophrenia and mental retardation, had been in the care of state hospital workers when they handed her a bus ticket home to Del Rio, Texas, on December 20. Three days later, she was found dead. According to the *Express-News* article, two teenagers walking along railroad tracks east of downtown near Walters Street and Runnels Avenue found her facedown in a watery concrete ditch.

"Her death raises questions about how state psychiatric hospitals release patients and highlights a little-known practice of leaving many at bus depots to find their way home," the article stated. *The Express-News* reported that according to state records, nearly six hundred patients discharged from the San Antonio State Hospital had been dropped off at the bus station since January 2008.

The *Express-News* also reported that Bob Arizpe, the San Antonio State Hospital superintendent, said no employees had been disciplined as a result of the incident. The staff member who dropped Raquel off had last seen her standing in line for the bus. The superintendent also stated, "the only requirement we have is to get them to their mode of transportation." A Texas state senator said Padilla's death was horrifying. "Obviously this is a person who had serious mental illness and needed help," he said. "If the hospital administrators decided that workers broke no rules, then the rules need to be changed. If they don't do it by rules, then we will have to do it by changing the law."

Thank you to the *Express-News* for bringing this event before the public. Hopefully, the authorities change this method of discharging patients.

Insulin Shock Therapy Unit

Many patients were enrolled in regular insulin shock therapy. The insulin was administered intravenously. Patients were tied down on a cot and covered with a heavy ducting type material. Once they were secured to the cot, they were injected with large amounts of insulin. The purpose was to make the patient go into shock and have seizures and convulsions.

Patients chosen for this treatment were given smaller doses in the initial treatments and then gradually given larger doses to cause shock. Usually around 5:00 a.m. attendants and nurses would begin to round up patients who had been selected for the insulin shock therapy. Many were brought in from other male wards. Female patients received insulin shock therapy in the female ward. Treatments were the same for both sexes.

A doctor ordered various doses of insulin to be injected. The doses were very large compared to doses of patients who were administered insulin for other reasons, including diabetes. Diabetic patients were never included in this type of insulin therapy.

The heavy ducting type material covering the patient was strapped around the entire bed and held the patient securely to the bed. The patient's head and arms stuck out of the covering. Soon after the insulin was administered, the patient would go into convulsions and sweat profusely. The doctor and nurse watched the patient very closely until the desired convulsion was obtained. Convulsions usually occurred within an hour, sometimes sooner. After the insulin treatment, a dose of glucose was then administered through the patient's vein or a feeding tube inserted into the patient's nose. The glucose quickly stopped the convulsions, and the patient went to sleep.

Some patients were given a strong sugar mixture with orange juice to help bring them out of the insulin treatment. Once the ducting was removed and the sweat was wiped away from the patient's body, sometimes the patient would lay in the bed for several hours. When the patient could stand and walk, he or she was directed into a nearby shower. The patient then got dressed and was placed in a sitting room to relax until he or she was able to return to his or her designated ward. In a week, this process started all over and continued for at least six weeks until the "desired results" were obtained.

Most of the staff could not see any remarkable change in these patients' mental conditions after insulin therapy. For eight hours following treatment, patients were very confused and spoke very little. They slowly regained their composure, and the next day most of them were back to their normal hospital routine.

During my tenure, three patients died from insulin therapy. This type of "treatment" was discontinued in the late '50s or early '60s, mainly because of a newly hired hospital superintendent, Dr. Bennett. Dr. Bennett also banned several other treatments like the prefrontal lobotomy that seemed to have a high mortality rate.

The Prefrontal Lobotomy

The prefrontal lobotomy seemed to me unusually cruel to patients. Lobotomies were performed in the hospital during most of the 1950s. A patient scheduled for lobotomy would spend the night in the clinic operating room then be carted into surgery the next morning. Once in the operation theater, attendants held him or her down on the table. The nurses placed a rolled paper gag in the patient's mouth, between the upper and lower teeth. This preparation was done before a doctor attached electrodes to the temporal area of the brain and administered a shock. The patient then began to convulse and became unconscious immediately.

During the convulsion phase of the surgery, the doctor placed a spike type of instrument directly under the patient's eyelid in a small area at the top of the eye socket. There was a small indention just above the eye socket where the doctor would hammer the spike into the skull and then into the prefrontal area of the brain. The spike, which resembled a sharp nail about six or eight inches in length, was passed through this region and forcefully struck with a hammer to drive the spike into the skull. Once the spike was in the prefrontal area of the brain, the doctor moved the spike in a swooping motion to destroy parts of the prefrontal area of the brain.

The patient was in shock and convulsing the entire time the procedure was being performed. Staff members secured the patient to the operating table until the convulsions and surgery were complete. After the doctor was satisfied that the prefrontal portion of the brain was swooped, the patient was taken to the hospital clinic to recover (or in many cases to die).

I was told by one of the doctors that sometimes the damage to the prefrontal area of the brain caused a massive hemorrhage, thus killing the patient. The last lobotomy case I assisted with ended this way. I had known this patient, a young man in his late twenties who had resided on Ward 12. He had been confined to the criminal ward because of his extremely combative attitude and continual fighting with other patients and hospital staff. Many times he had been uncontrollable and had to be restrained. In order to neutralize his psychotic episodes, many aggressive shock treatments had been administered.

According to the medical staff, the shock treatments had not been successful, and other treatments became necessary, including the prefrontal lobotomy. I was told that "James" had been a medical student who became mentally ill and was committed to the hospital by the courts. He had resided on Ward 12 ever since his admission and later lived in the clinic, where he died from complications of the lobotomy. As far as I knew, this was the last lobotomy ever performed at the hospital.

I had the opportunity to work with and supervise several other patients who received lobotomies. Most who survived went into a "vegetable" state, and they had no real quality of life. The criminal ward patients who received lobotomies were transferred to a lower security ward. They no longer needed strict observation, as the effects of the lobotomy calmed most of them. The lobotomy was the final treatment, and if patients survived, most did not even know their own names. Post-treatment therapy for lobotomy patients was conducted by hospital therapists and began on a kindergarten level. These patients seemed to peak at an adolescent level of performance once they recovered.

This procedure ended when at last the state hired a new hospital superintendent, Dr. E.W. Bennett, a retired fifty-five year old military psychiatrist. Col. Bennett was a true Christian who instilled a kinder influence on the entire staff and seemed to have more interest in the patients than did his predecessor. Dr. Bennett and his wife resided in a large mansion directly in front of the Administration Building.

When Dr. Bennett became the hospital superintendent, he immediately chose a qualified clinical director for the hospital to replace the previous clinical director. Together, the new superintendent and the new clinical director gave an order to cease all insulin shock therapy and the prefrontal lobotomies within the hospital. This marked a turning point for the hospital, making it a much more effective treatment center for the mentally ill.

The Advent of Tranquilizers

In the late '50s, new drugs were made available to the hospital to treat all types of mental illness. Thorazine, phenothiazines, chlorpromazine, prochlorperazine, and reserpine all became the "penicillin" for treatment of mental illness. Most resident patients were placed on some form of these drugs.

We could see that it helped patients with anxiety and hallucination problems. Patients seemed to be relieved of all types of disturbances and were able to sleep at night and remain calm during the day. The use of the new form of tranquilizers soon changed the treatment phase, which had included giving patients high doses of barbiturates. Patients were treated with tranquilizers for such illnesses as acute and chronic schizophrenia; manic depression; and paranoid disturbances. We noticed tranquilizers also were useful in treating anxiety, tension, agitation, aggression, and destructiveness.

With the advent of the tranquilizers, treatments such as insulin therapy and shock therapy could be reduced or ceased. However, in some cases physicians combined shock therapy and tranquilizers. With the new tranquilizers, many patients were reachable by the staff the first time.

So widely prescribed were these medications that the pills were sent to the hospital in five gallon barrels. The pharmacy then distributed them to patient wards.

Drastic Changes in Weather Caused Havoc at the Hospital

Prior to tranquilizer treatments, changes in weather and, believe it or not, a full moon brought on unrest at the hospital. The hospital kept records of the moon phases, and it was a proven fact that a full moon had a great deal to do with patients' actions. Many patients became disturbed and very unruly.

I remember that upon arriving for my shift after a full moon or change in weather, the staff would report that most patients had been restless all night. The full moon also seemed to cause disturbances among many of the patients. Some had to have an emergency shock administered to calm them down.

Once tranquilizers became available, they usually had a good effect on most of these patients. The wards became quiet and patients seemed to rest easily.

Chapter 7

Working on the Criminal Ward

On day two of my new job, I checked in, obtained my set of keys, and proceeded to Ward 12. On the walkway to the ward, I heard a lot of yelling, cursing, and crying from the wards as I passed.

When I arrived at my assigned destination, Mr. Lee told me that the weather had changed and a storm was approaching. He also stated that a change in the weather always caused the patients to become restless and that I would notice an increase of noise among the patients.

That explained why the patients had been making so much noise as I walked to the ward. In fact, the night shift attendants reported that most of the patients had stayed awake most of the night and were rowdy and restless. They had given Mr. Lee a list of the patients who were "disturbed" so he could report it to the ward doctor, who would be making rounds later in the morning.

Today being shock day, the attendants were told to move about thirty beds together in the big dorm for the shock treatments. We chose roughly twelve patients to move the beds and prepare for the doctor and nurse to arrive.

Mr. Lee had in his hand a list of patients who were to be shocked that morning. The doctor never questioned anyone's name on the list. We went out onto the porch, called the patients' names, and instructed them to lie in the beds that had been prepared. Most of the patients who were called came freely and took their spot in the designated bed. A couple had to be restrained and brought forcibly.

The doctor, Dr. M, and Nurse Jane arrived with a black box that was the shock machine. Mr. Lee had prepared some mouth gags to be used to protect the patients as they convulsed after receiving the shocks. Dr. M quickly began to attach electrodes to the head of first patient. Two attendants, one on each side of the bed, held the patient down and the doctor pushed the button. The patient went into convulsions and began to tremble. Then he made a loud noise like a scream. It was all over in a few seconds. The first patient had been treated.

In private hospitals, sedatives were usually administered for this procedure, but not here. In this mental hospital, the doctor simply moved on to the next patient and proceeded to administer the electrical shock. It took about forty-five minutes to finish all the prescribed treatments.

It seemed strange to me that neither the doctor nor the nurse talked to any of the patients; they never advised them what was going to happen. This procedure seemed to be a common practice at the hospital during this time. When the doctor and nurse left the ward, the first patient began to wake and talk. The attendants told the patient to just lay back, rest, and enjoy the rest of the day. Most patients urinated on their clothing during the convulsions, then were in a daze and appeared lifeless for several hours. Some, however, woke immediately and were escorted to the showers to change clothing.

I later learned that shock treatments were administered one day a week. Most of the recipients remained calm for the whole day. Some remained calm for the rest of the week. Throughout the treatment process, the patients waiting on the porch were restless, wondering if they would be the next to receive shock treatment. After the doctor and nurse left the ward, the untouched patients began to settle down.

Bus Transfer of Some Criminal Patients to Another Hospital

One late afternoon, about 2 years into my tenure, some staff members were told that about forty male patients from the criminal ward would be transferred to another hospital. Rusk State Hospital was an old prison system facility that provided more security. Not many staff members knew of the decision to make the transfer. Patients were not told prior to or during the trip where they were going.

Around 6:00 a.m. on the chosen day, we were to load the selected criminal patients directly on a chartered bus for transfer. That morning, we told all forty patients to get dressed and then placed a leather belt with leather hand restraints onto each of them. We gave the patients prescribed sedatives in order to calm them for the trip. Tranquilizers had just become available during the time of the patient transfers.

Rusk State Hospital was about 150 miles north of San Antonio. It was surrounded by a double chain-link fence with electric gates. I was sure some of the more alert patients had a shock at seeing the gates open by themselves for the bus to enter. Two state police cars escorted the bus the entire trip. Of course, there needed to be a couple of pit stops along the way. The police blocked off the road until the patients had a chance to relieve themselves at the side of the road. Fortunately, there were no real problems inside the bus or during the pit stops. About a dozen uniformed attendants from the hospital were present on the bus. With the police escort, we were able to travel very fast to the new destination.

A Patient Was Transferred to the Rusk State Hospital

On a separate occasion, one early morning, the hospital medical staff asked me and another technician to take a male patient to the Rusk State Hospital. I will call the patient Fret. He was about fifty-five years old and weighed about 150 pounds.

Fret was a con artist and had used his talents to swindle many folks out of their savings. He always had a good story to tell the victims about how he could make them a lot of money. He never did anything but take the money and run. He was very convincing and could easily make people think he was truthful.

He had been committed to the state hospital as a mental patient later on in his life. He resided on Ward 12 for about a year. The superintendent felt that Fret was a flight risk and should be sent to a place where he could not escape. That place was Rusk State Hospital.

During our trip to the other hospital, we drove in our personal vehicle. Fret rode in the backseat and was restrained with a belt around his waist and cuffs on his arms. The staff doctor had given Fret a shot to calm him and cause him to sleep while we traveled.

All went well until he woke up and wanted to use a restroom. We stopped at a service station and took him into the bathroom so he could relieve himself.

When we were ready to travel on, Fret yelled to the station operator that he was being kidnapped. We had to assure the operator at the station that Fret was a mental patient and that we were transferring him to another hospital. We were wearing white shirts, pants, and black ties, which probably convinced the station operator that we were on a legitimate mission.

The rest of the trip went well until we drove up to the wire gates at the hospital. Then Fret offered us a couple of nice diamonds he said were hidden near his home. All we had to do was open the vehicle door and let him walk away. Of course, we ignored him and proceeded into the walls of the hospital. That was the last time we saw him.

The Hospital Parade

During the late spring or early summertime, all the staff designed and built pretty floats that they then drove within the hospital grounds as part of a parade. This was always an interesting sight, and patients participated. All patients who had outside-of-ward privileges were involved. The parade was a big event. The hospital volunteer council members attended and rode the parade route.

It was good entertainment for the closed-ward patients as well. They were encouraged to go to the porches and watch through the grates. Patients would cheer and yell at the participants from their ward porches. People riding the floats threw candy out to bystanders just like in parades seen in cities and towns.

Chapter 8

My Study as a Psychiatric Technician

After my first three months as an attendant, I registered for school at the hospital and through San Antonio College. The college had connected with the hospital for regular subjects such as microbiology, introduction to psychology, chemistry, English, and Texas government. My uniform changed to a white buttoned jacket; this was the dress for physicians and other therapists at the hospital.

Classes in pharmacology, anatomy and physiology, surgery, psychiatric studies, nursing arts, and chemistry were all taught at the hospital. The instructors were staff physicians and other hospital medical staff. In all, there were approximately twelve medical doctors on staff and one clinical director. The superintendent of the hospital was also a psychiatrist. Most of the physicians were also psychiatrists or at least studying psychiatry. A lot of the staff doctors had trained in Mexico or Cuba and had come to the United States for work.

Several doctors arrived from Cuba during this time; they had escaped the Castro takeover. In need of more physicians, the state hospital had quickly hired the new foreign doctors. Many hardly spoke English; however, this did not create a problem since many patients were of Mexican descent and spoke Spanish.

Some of the new doctors who arrived from various other countries were not licensed in the United States or even in Texas. However, several were well-qualified physicians and godsends to the hospital and the patients. Even though some of the new physicians could not speak English very well, their skills were noticed and patients benefited from their service to the medical team.

The state hospital was also a good fit for some Texas licensed doctors who evidently could not make it in a normal hospital setting or private practice due to their drug addictions or mental problems. A team of staff doctors began to offer rehabilitation therapy in private to any doctors who wished to avail themselves of treatment. Eventually, most of the doctors became adjusted to the new environment and a good number were indeed an asset to the hospital. Others were discharged from duty and left the hospital.

At any one time, there were about twelve doctors on the staff, plus several medical students doing their rotations. Texas law required all doctors applying for Texas licenses to take a course in Texas government before they were tested. Staff doctors rotated night shifts, and at least one doctor was on call at the hospital during weekends and holidays.

A Female Staff Doctor Was a Kidnapper

It is interesting how easy it was for doctors to obtain employment back in the early 1950s. One female doctor who worked on the staff for several years was written up in the *Saturday Evening Post* or *Life* magazine. She had evidently kidnapped a young child in a hospital in New Mexico, then fled to San Antonio and was hired as a ward physician at the State Hospital.

One day while I was in the admissions and supervisors office, a patient came in holding a magazine with a photo of Dr. Campbell on the cover. The whole story was printed therein. It shocked the entire office staff. The doctor soon left the hospital and we never heard anything about her again. This issue was the talk of the entire hospital staff. Most were baffled as to how she had been hired in the first place.

The Student Nurses

The hospital was a certified teaching facility for student nurses. These students were required to study psychiatry in order to receive their affiliation with the Texas Board of Nurse Examiners.

The student nurses came to San Antonio from all across Texas. They remained at the hospital for at least six weeks during their studies. Staff physicians introduced them to psychiatry through hands-on study. Every three months, a new group of student nurses was assigned to the hospital. The student nurses had already successfully completed most of their academic study in their respective hometown hospitals and colleges. Psychiatric study was their final schooling prior to returning home. Their examinations for the Texas Board of Nurse Examiners were next. Then they were licensed professional nurses.

Beginning my in-house study and working with the student nurses was like a breath of fresh air. In the main office, as part of my study and work, I was able to meet and work with them. After I had been on the staff for about two years, I met a beautiful student nurse and began dating her after hours. She left the hospital and went to a pediatric hospital in Dallas to continue her required studies. We corresponded while she was located in Dallas. When she graduated from the school of nursing in Abilene, I traveled there to visit her. We were soon married in Abilene, Texas.

We set up our home in San Antonio. She was employed at the Baptist Memorial Hospital as an emergency room nurse. After about a year, we moved into the state hospital employee housing. We soon began our family while I continued working at the state hospital, and she began working part time. She worked on weekends while I kept the children at our home. Our family grew at the state hospital; we had five children while we resided there. They were all delivered at Baptist Memorial Hospital by our personal physicians.

The state hospital facilities were humble, but they were furnished and the rent was very low. Also, all the utilities and laundry were furnished by the hospital. I was soon promoted to the Hospital Rehabilitation Department after graduating from the psychotherapy technician program. We were then given a larger home as soon as it became available.

For this book, I contacted several student nurses who are now registered professional nurses to provide comments about their observations while they were students at the hospital. I have inserted comments from at least four of these former students below. I would like to extend my thanks to the nurses, as they wrote from a different perspective.

Jerry Beauchamp

B.L.P., RN

We arrived as senior nurse students in the fall of 1953 to study the teachings of Sigmund Freud for three months.

Freud believed that patients' complaints proved to be caused by unconscious conflicts over desires they had in childhood. He stated that in a normal sex life no neurosis is possible. He believed that mental illness could be cured by psychoanalysis.

Even if this is true, how it could have worked with three thousand patients? I remember being taught that a cold mother causes schizophrenia. It did not make sense to me then and still doesn't.

The class before us told of a gypsy fortune-teller with amazing powers, and we quickly sought her out. We lived on the grounds, and she was easy to find. She was dressed in colorful clothes and had a wild look in her eyes. One by one she told us alarming predictions of our futures. To this day, when I see Dee, she asks me to check her skin for jaundice. I try to assure her that at the age of eighty, the prediction of her dying of liver cancer has probably expired.

I was assigned to the women's dorm my first week. We were to choose one patient with whom to interact and observe. I can still see her today. She was about forty-five years old with a sweet disposition and was glad to have my attention. She seemed normal in every way, and I was anxious to hear her story. She came from a wealthy family, and her mother and father had died, leaving money and jewels. Her sister, in effort to take all the money, had her committed. We both cried as we discussed the injustice of the system.

On Friday, I spent my day at the Administration Building where the patients' medical records were housed. I began reading the charts as I was anxious to learn about her. As I read her personal information, to my amazement it listed her as an only child coming from a family of meager means. My first lesson taught me that, with the mentally ill, nothing is as it seems.

My second lesson came when I realized there is nothing crazier than a sick crazy person. Barb and I were assigned to the clinic in the men's wing. We had about twelve patients with different medical diagnoses like pneumonia and infections. We always had guys from the base who worked on their days off help us except for this one day. We were it; there were no hospital personnel available except for an emergency. We made rounds, fed them, and gave them their meds. We went to the room of a patient who was unable to walk; he had severe dementia and a diagnosis of diarrhea. He was in a terrible mess. There were no adult diapers in the '50s, and he had BM from head to toe. To pass the time, he had stuffed it in his ears and under the mattress. We did not think a washcloth would work well. There were no showers, but we located a tub down the hall, and with difficulty we loaded him into a wheelchair, filled the tub, and dumped him in. He laughed and had a great time until it came time to get him out of the tub and we realized we could not lift him over the edge. After many tries, we tied a sheet around his waist and hauled him into the wheelchair and then into to a nice clean bed for a nap.

At the end of the hall was a large room with five men with varied problems. They were glad to see pretty young girls and welcomed us with whistles and cheers and compliments on our looks and bedside manners. We were aware of how much they enjoyed their bed baths. After completing all the morning assignments, we went on rounds before lunch. Upon approaching the room of the patient with the gastrointestinal problems, our noses told us that not at all was well. He had not had that nice long nap we had hoped. We watched in horror as we saw him again playing in his poop. We looked at each other and began to cry. After we regained our composure, we started to laugh, all the while rolling up our sleeves and getting back to work. What a day! No wonder I remember as if it were yesterday.

We were assigned to a room that held a good-looking twenty-six-year-old med student. He was charming and well mannered. He had been home from college for the summer and working at his dad's gas station when something triggered a psychotic episode, and he fought the customers and his family. His family sought help, and the doctor suggested a new procedure called a lobotomy. My classmate and I had observed the procedure, and it reminded us of our science labs where they pithed frogs.

Something that looked like an ice pick was pushed into the brain above the eyes, and they met in the middle and cut nerve fibers. The patients I observed after the procedure were childlike; only some of them could still feed themselves. The hope was that it would destroy the part of the brain that was responsible for aggression and they could live at home peaceably. Remember that in the '50s there were no psychotic drugs of any kind. We only had phenobarbital and warm baths to calm the agitated. They both helped to some extent, but the drug made them sleepy. In desperation, the family agreed to the lobotomy. As the time neared, we became frantic, but since we were student nurses, no one would listen to us. On the morning of surgery, we decided between the two of us to chart an elevated temperature because no one operated on a patient with fever. It bought him a few days, but the following week he had his surgery and died of an infection a week later.

There were no Mayo educated doctors working at San Antonio for the small pay the state allowed. But then, they were also trying this new procedure in the best hospitals. President Kennedy's sister had a lobotomy with tragic results.

Thursday was electric shock day. The patients were aware, and anxiety was in the air. Our job as students was to catch the patients and take them to the treatment room. It all reminded me of when I was a child and they sent me in the chicken coop to catch dinner. We did have a coat hanger with a hook on the end, but with the patients all we could do was chase and hold.

We placed them on the table in the treatment room, and each student would hold a limb to keep them from getting up while the doctor placed the electrodes on their heads and administered the shock. The legislature spent so little on the mentally ill that there was no money for sedating IV medication like was given in regular hospitals. Afterward, we would wheel them into a room and wait for them to wake. It was the only treatment we did that seemed to work for the severely depressed, and it is still used in some hospitals today.

On Wednesday, the Budweiser Band came and played for a dance. The patients spent the day getting ready and loved to go to the dance. The women would dress in their finest and decorate their hair with ribbons. Their sense of fashion always brought smiles to our faces. We were responsible for mingling with the men. Buffalo loved to dance. He had been there most of his life. He was mentally delayed and thought he was five years old when in reality he was sixty. He loved the students and would bring us pecans, and in return he would ask us to comb his hair with a comb he kept in his blue overall pocket. He always had a red bandana around his neck.

There was a court-ordered alcoholic dorm. It was against the law in Texas to be a vagrant, so they were picked up and brought to dry out for three months. They mostly smoked and played dominos and took care of themselves.

We had some criminally insane, and some of the students had ambivalent feelings after hearing their sides of the story. I remember an especially charming man who was accused of raping two sisters in the same bed at the same time. Some could not see how this could happen and thought the sisters were saving themselves from their daddy's wrath. As I look back, maybe he had a knife.

Many patients were allowed the freedom to roam the hospital grounds. Sometimes they were walking to work or running errands for the staff. We were told to keep an eye out for them. They were bad about taking a willing lady, or a willing lady taking them, behind a building for time alone. Birth control was yet in the future, and it could turn out to be a big problem.

Dee and I were assigned to insulin shock therapy; the theory being that the coma from large doses of insulin would shock the mind out of depression. We went to work at 5:00 a.m. and prepared the patients for their treatments. We gave large doses of insulin according to their weight and carefully watched as the coma was induced. Just before they went too far into unconsciousness, we placed tubes through their noses into their stomachs and poured syrup to awaken them. They would then take showers, and we would go to breakfast. Dee and I still talk about this very pretty thirty-year-old lady who we would help shower, and she always used perfume with the most wonderful scent. Just last year I found the perfume in a vintage catalog and sent a bottle to Dee. It was called Hope.

We look back and recall the bad things, but when I see a poor soul lying on the sidewalk, talking to the wind, I wish for a beautiful place of safe refuge like the San Antonio State Hospital with huge pecan trees and grass to sit on for a quick rest. There he would get three meals a day and a clean bed at night. He would have a job on the farm or in the kitchen. He could play pool or baseball, and on Wednesday night he could dance to the Budweiser Band. There would be a kind staff doing their best with the knowledge they had at the time. He might even have a student nurse to give him a good bath. Have we learned anything? Is turning them out on the street to sleep under bridges a better way sixty years later?

I loved my time at the state hospital and have wondered what in my personality made this so. The people were funny, sweet, and sad. Perhaps a simpler reason could have been the fun weekends spent doing the town with the guys from the three air force bases and one army base.

S.S., Student Nurse and later RN and Employee

It was quite challenging to work with patients who were both physically and mentally ill, as some were very disturbed and ended up in locked rooms. To give them medications, I had to take an attendant with me. We received patients from other state mental hospitals as well. We were always understaffed, but the psychiatric nurse technicians rotated through the clinic, and that helped. While I was there, I set up a medication room to better organize the system and assigned student nurses to give out the medications. The existing system was ancient. Our house doctor was a retired army man (Dr. Franz). I don't know what he did all day, but exactly at 3:00 p.m., when I was to go off my shift, he would appear and want to make rounds. This delay took an extra hour and caused me to be on overtime every day.

The worst memory I have working at the clinic was undoubtedly the day I scrubbed in for a lobotomy done by Dr. Franz. (He seemed to enjoy doing these procedures.) The procedure was, to me, so horrible and cruel, and under the primitive surgical conditions, it was risky to say the least. (The patient died later from infections.) As far as the lobotomy is concerned, I understood why they were done. The surgical procedure was the last option to control "violent" mental patients. They did not have the medications available then as they do now. The hospital did not have the option of sending them back home and treating them in an out-patient facility.

Mental health medical treatment has come a long way since the 1950s. Also, medical care has improved even for the mentally ill.

I learned a lot at SASH the four months I was there as a student and then as an employee for another year as a registered nurse.

J.F., RN

One of the first things that I remember at SASH is the garden where they raised watermelons. I had my first watermelon rind preserves at the hospital. They were delicious. I remember the little man who saved Bull Durham tobacco sacks and the yellow string and then made himself two complete suits to wear. I only got to see him once.

The insulin shock contained precise instructions for such young, inexperienced nurses while I was a student at the hospital. The body cover used during the treatment could have been canvas that we put over the patients and used to tie them down to the bed. The insulin was administered at a very early hour in the morning. We monitored their stages of treatment, and then when they went into shock, a stomach tube was placed through the nose into the stomach. A sugar solution was poured into the tube in hope of bringing them out of shock. Every response was different; some patients were difficult to tube, and, of course if not done quickly, they would convulse and might die. So scary. We were so thankful when the treatment was over and the patient was responsive again. I remember that removing the canvas covers from the bodies of the patients was very smelly from the excess perspiration from the insulin reaction.

Our exposure to electric shock had been very humane at the hospital where I trained (Hendricks). There, the doctor would bring a black box to the unit and leave it outside the room as he made rounds. The doctor would visit with the patients at length and then administer an IV solution. The box was brought in after the patient was asleep, and then the shock treatment was given.

At the state hospital, patients were rounded up in groups in one large room. False teeth were removed, and their pockets were emptied. These patients were so nervous and frightened as they waited their turn for a shock. This was not a pleasant part of my job.

One of the times that I was anxious was when taking patients to the hospital dance. They checked the patients out of the ward with two student nurses; one led the single file line through the dark to the building where the dance was held. The other student brought up the rear of the line of patients. I am sure we had forty or fifty patients in the line.

When the dance was over, we took them back the same way we brought them, except it was very dark, very little light. The patients were then checked back into the ward for the rest of the night. I don't think we would have known if one or more of the patients had decided to skip out of the line. Yes, we got to dance too.

We made cotton swabs on the ward. We had small sticks and cotton. I think we did a pretty good job even though they did not resemble Q-tips. At church on Sunday we took a long line to the building where the dance was held previously. It was a Catholic service, and all the patients drank from the same communion cup.

At the class study, I remember the study of the various facets of mental illness and the symptoms or manifestations related to each. I thought that even normal people had some of these characteristics. We were told that. Then we were asked to write down the name of someone in every group in whom one or two characteristics had been noted. I think they all wrote about me and branded me as paranoid. I was embarrassed, but such is life.

E.C., RN

In 1964, I was a student nurse at the San Antonio State Hospital for six weeks. I had been looking forward to the experience before I arrived there because I wanted to get a degree in psychology eventually. At the end of the six weeks, I hated the experience, but after getting my RN degree, I still wanted to get a degree in psychology. Although after I got a few hours through a correspondence class, I never finished my goal in psychology. My first impression was that of much sadness for very ill patients who never had a visitor at the state hospital. There were few staff, but the ones that were there worked very hard and did the best they could.

Touring the "cages" with dirt floors that many people were put into was pure devastation for me. I was so very glad when they were no longer used at the state hospital. My most memorable experience was that every morning at the beginning of classes, our female instructor had us sing “You are My Sunshine.” We made fun of her for it, but as I have matured, I understand why she had us sing it.

My best experience was the patient conference sessions where the physicians reviewed several cases. Also, I really enjoyed the dancing and games sessions with the more stable patients.

My worst experiences were with patient case studies where we had to interview and interact with the more severe patients who lived in locked-up quarters. Since then, I will not go into any locked area. When visiting places that have mocked-up jails, I cannot even step into the cell even though I know the door will not be closed.

The electroshock therapy and insulin shock therapy were another of my worst experiences. My fear was that I would not properly care for the patient in post-therapy, and I disliked having to hold down the patient during electroshock. Having been there only six weeks, I was not sure that either treatment really helped them.

Another experience I had was that my father’s father was committed to the state hospital. I am not sure of the year. It had to be in the late 1940s. My mother talked of his being committed as a horrible thing for his wife to do to him. She thought he must have had a stroke, but I was not able to find out why he was committed. I never really pursued it because my mother always became very upset when the subject was brought up. She referred to this experience many times, only saying how cruel it was. I am not even sure if she even visited him.

Working at Southeast Baptist Hospital, I had a male employee who worked part time in the middle ’90s at the state hospital as a nurse’s aide. He really liked his experience with the patients and said the conditions had gotten better, but still inadequacy abounded in many cases. Every time I drive near the hospital, I am reminded of my experiences there.

Psychiatric Technician Program

The psychiatric technician program was tailored after the nurse’s education program, except the technician program was focused on mental illness. The course was a twenty-four month hands-on study.

The first graduating class contained forty students. The program was in connection with the San Antonio College and both the college and the Board for State Hospitals and Special Schools certified the graduates. Prior to this program, no professional study had been available at the mental hospital.

At some time in the past, the hospital did do some training with nursing students. Also, ten or fifteen years prior to the technician program, the hospital had conducted a nurse graduate program. However, the graduate program was never approved by the State College Board, therefore it was discontinued. More than one hundred graduates finished the program before it was abandoned.

The new psychiatric technician program started in the late 1950s gave these students pay as they worked and studied medical courses. Even though the pay was small, it helped folks who could not otherwise afford college. The schooling was adequate, allowing students to work directly with the mental patients. The technicians were authorized to give medications, draw blood, and properly keep medical charts on patients. This was a new and much-needed service in mental health treatment.

During the year of 1954, the hospital was serving between 2,800 and 3,000 male and female patients. At that time the hospital had a full-time staff of more than eight hundred employees. Opportunities for professional education were offered by the hospital for persons preparing for positions as nurses, psychiatric technicians, occupational therapists, recreation therapists, industrial therapists, psychologists, and pastoral caregivers.

The psychiatric nurse technician program started in 1954 and continued for almost a decade. The psychiatric technician program provided sixty-one hours of college credit and a certificate of successful completion. It also provided a diploma from San Antonio College.

Upon graduation, the graduates were assigned throughout the hospital as supervisors directly serving the patients. This program was the result of the state of Texas and the San Antonio State Hospital managers. The state was concerned about developing well-trained personnel and provided this program to help meet the increased need for more adequately trained personnel in the field of psychiatric nursing. The desired type of students was selected.

The hospital furnished adequate training so that the graduates could adequately share in the large load of patient population.

To be successful, the program had to develop a student's ability to identify behavior patterns and provide for all the patients' needs. Graduates of the program were provided emotionally secure guidance so they could meet any psychotic problem and know how to treat patients. The graduates strived to provide a harmonious understanding between the technician and their co-workers, thus providing a better therapeutic team.

The graduates developed the ability to encourage patients to assume more socially acceptable patterns of behavior. The overall program was focused on establishing an understanding of treatment relationships and responsibilities as well as becoming an informed citizen.

Normal Personality According to Dr. Jackson

Dr. Jackson, a staff psychiatric physician, outlined the "normal personality" at a meeting of the San Antonio State Hospital Psychiatric Nurse Technicians on September 14, 1964:

> One must achieve a feeling of self-security and self-esteem *without exaggeration*_in either direction; work fruitfully and gain *satisfaction* from work; maintain a pleasant and adequate relationship with colleagues; be able to give and accept love from a suitable partner and have a satisfactory sexual relationship with his or her mate.
>
> He or she has intimate friends of the same sex. A well-rounded life should contain a gratifying avocation, such as a sport or hobby. A person must be capable of self-criticism and examination, not setting a standard that is too high. Neither should one be too compulsive of his or her behavior. The normal person is ambitious but not to excess. He or she must not turn each failure into a tragedy. We must be able to take orders from supervisors and to give them to inferiors without hostility or resentment.

This person must be able to understand a fair amount of loss without guilt or excessive anxiety.

Study Outline and Facts and Figures Concerning the Hospital

At a meeting of the student technicians in 1964, Ms. Sarah Hazard, RN and director of the education psychiatric technician program at the San Antonio State Hospital, provided an outline for study:

Outline of the Study for the Psychiatric Technician Program

- Studying
- Planning
- Concentrating
- Reading
- Taking Notes
- Memorizing
- Reviewing
- Taking Examinations
- Graduation Diploma
- Assignment to various departments of the hospital as psychiatric technician (certified by the Boards for State Hospitals and Special Schools)

At the same meeting, Ms. Amy Burrows, RN and assistant hospital nursing director, spoke and provided a handout detailing the following stats concerning the daily operation of the hospital during the year of 1964:

The Supply Section of the Hospital

Our hospital presently (1955) has a population of over 2,800 patients. Our bed space according to the American Psychiatric Association is no more than 2344 patients; hence, any number beyond this (2344) is overcrowding. The San Antonio State Hospital is the second largest and the second oldest of six state hospitals. Austin, Texas has the oldest and largest population. Other state hospitals for the mentally ill are located in Austin, Terrell, Rusk, Wichita Falls, Big Spring, and Kerrville. At this time, the San Antonio State Hospital has 900 employees; 500 of this amount are in nursing services. Our male and female populations are close to 1400 patients each. The clothing allowance per patient is only $9.75. Our state appropriation is approximately $3.91 per patient per day. This amount includes salaries of employees, food, medication, clothing, utilities, and maintenance of the physical plant. Our food and preparation allotment is 81 cents per patient each day or 27 cents per meal per patient. Raw food allotment is 58 cents per day or 19 and 1/3 cents per meal.

Food service prepares and serves more than 261,000 meals per month and 3,140,000 meals per year. Food service prepares and serves more than 1,500 patients at one time in the big dining room; 2,000 meals are served each mealtime from the state hospital kitchen. Meals served to the patients provide adequate calories, vitamin content, and mineral content. There are seventy buildings on the hospital grounds. Five hundred and fifty-eight acres are allocated to the hospital. The main hospital complex is comprised of 106 acres.

There are many cases that are contributing factors in producing mental illnesses. In many cases there is no one cause. A person is not born with mental illness. It develops from an ineffectual attempt to cope with one's problems or to adjust to environmental demands.

Not all patients receive electroshock therapy (EST). Such treatment is determined individually. Patients who are financially able are expected to pay for their hospitalization. This is required only in cases where it causes no hardship to the family. All patients receive the same care and consideration whether they are able to pay or not. Most of our patients do not pay for their hospitalization. No one except those whose duty it is to determine costs and to collect know who is a paying patient, and it is not made public.

Patients are referred to rehabilitation therapies by their ward physicians. Most of the wards are overcrowded at all times. The average stay for new admissions or length of hospitalization is sixty to ninety days. The hospital has an average of at least twelve admissions per day, of which 55 percent are voluntary. Approximately a year ago only 35 percent of the admissions were voluntary. The average stay of patients in this state hospital during April 1964 was one year and eleven days. In May 1964, the entire state hospital system had a population of 15,796. (In May 1964, the San Antonio State Hospital had 460 patients in excess of rated bed capacity as determined by the American Psychiatric Association.)

The canteen or little store is for the patients and employees. The beauty shop and barber shop facilities are free to all patients and considered a therapeutic and hygienic value. So is the shoe shop. According to 1960 figures, our medical center and clinic cost about a third of a million dollars. The outpatient facility cost $100,000. The rehabilitation building cost $200,000. The mattress shop cost $20,000.

Five new elevators have been installed. They are located in Wards O, L, and 14—male and female wards (1964). Several wards and buildings have been completely renovated in the last two years. Several are now being remodeled. The roads on the grounds have been rebuilt under contract by the Texas Highway Department. The sewage system has been enlarged and repaired. The heating system has been modernized.

1960 Figures and Estimates

- Our electric bill is about $4,000 per month.
- The water bill is about $1,400 per month.
- The telephone bill is about $1,700 per month.
- The gas bill is about $3,000 per month.
- The sewage bill is about $500 per month.

The supply section is responsible to the business manager for purchasing all supplies used by this institution. Supplies are usually ordered on a quarterly basis. Approximately $200,000 worth of supplies is kept in our warehouse at all times. These supplies consist of food, cleaning supplies, drugs, office supplies, plumbing supplies, electrical supplies, and hardware supplies. All supplies that are purchased are received and issued by our warehouse section, which consists of four warehousemen and one truck driver. The supply office consists of one supply officer, one assistant, two purchasing clerks, and two stock record clerks.

All suppliers are entered on stock record cards, and a requisition must be obtained from the different departments before an issue can be made. In addition to the regular stock items, a number of special items are purchased during the year. All requests for special items as well as stock items must be approved by the business manager of the hospital.

Chapter 9

Industrial Therapy Now Used to Treat Mental Illness

In 1954, after my graduation, I was chosen to begin a new therapy unit within the hospital. I was given the title of senior industrial therapist. This therapy oversaw all the patients who worked within the hospital.

Industrial therapy is akin to occupational therapy, with the exception that patients were assigned to work details within the hospital. Progress records were kept of the patients' responses and their work history. Until the Industrial Therapy Department began, patients had been randomly selected by ward attendants to perform work. But now, every patient who worked at any hospital chore was assigned to a position they were qualified to perform.

During my first year in this new position, interviews and training were performed by the Industrial Therapy Department. No longer would a patient be forced to work in an area when he or she might do better in another task. Approximately six hundred patients were interviewed, coached, and counseled for particular job assignments.

The Industrial Therapy Sheltered Workshop

The new superintendent, Dr. Bennett, saw the need for more workforce training for the patients. He chose me to enroll in a course of study in New York City in a school associated with New York University. This school was The Institute for the Crippled and Disabled.

I had never been to New York and was quite apprehensive about the new assignment. However, with the help of the superintendent, Dr. Bennett, I traveled to New York and began my study. After three weeks, the school gave me the certification of Prevocational Evaluation Supervisor. This was entirely new to Texas and the mental hospitals there. The first accredited patient evaluation for vocational training in Texas began at the San Antonio State Hospital.

When I returned to the hospital after visiting other states and their industrial therapy programs, I began to formulate a new industrial therapy unit known as a sheltered workshop. Now that we had the ability to test and choose patients for specialized work, I began to look for businesses outside the hospital that we could contract with. Our first successful contract was for the assembly of ballpoint pens.

We originally hired about six patients from the hospital patient registry. Each was tested with actual assembly of the pens. At first we paid the patients minimum wage, but after closer inspection, we found some couldn't perform the task at the same level a regular worker could. We then established a sliding scale for the patient based on the percentage of performance a normal individual would perform. Many had not earned a wage in as long as twenty years. Patients received these wages in in-house coupons that could be used like money.

This part of therapy in a sheltered workshop was the first in any Texas state mental hospital. This hospital became known nationwide for its new way to rehabilitate the mentally ill. Some of the in-house jobs included dining room attendant, farm attendant, creamery attendant, carpenter shop attendant, janitor, and laundry attendant. Some also worked off campus in housecleaning, mainly for employers who understood the patients' mental conditions. Some of these patients were eventually allowed to be picked up by others for work at private homes. The homes and residents were always screened, and we provided precautions for them and the patient. This worked very well, as many patients were able to leave the hospital for the day and return at night. Most, if not all, were still on medication and were able to function outside the hospital setting for the day.

The sheltered workshop was instrumental in training many patients. Many successful patients gained self-esteem that they would probably have never had the opportunity to gain elsewhere.

Our Hospital Patient Housekeeper

While I was in the rehabilitation center and in charge of the patients that were able to work, I met a nice older lady I'll call Margaret. Margaret was of German extraction and spoke English pretty well. She did our personal housecleaning. Margaret came almost every day to our house, walking to work from the hospital area. She was very trustworthy, and the children liked her very much. She in turn played with the children and became part of our extended family.

Margaret had been a patient for more than twenty years, and during that time she mostly just sat on the ward with not much to do. She never had visitors and seemed to be a lonely person. The housecleaning job was very rewarding to Margaret, and we appreciated it as well. We instilled in her a form of self-esteem. She never mentioned her family since she had left home for confinement at the hospital. We provided her with some spending money on a regular basis, and she was able to purchase items from the hospital store. She had never had that opportunity at the hospital prior to coming to work in our home.

Patients Who Earned a Vacation

Most of the workers in the sheltered workshop were given a vacation. Patients enjoyed extra treats, such as a visit to the inner city or a meal at a fast-food place, and they were all taken to a movie theater downtown. We made arrangements with the owner at the Majestic Theater for the patients to attend a movie for free. The patients were allowed to enter through the rear door of the theater, which was connected to the third-floor balcony. The entire balcony was reserved for these sheltered workshop mental patients. This was the highlight of the patients' vacation.

The selected patients from the sheltered workshop required little supervision. The staff members who were their trainers accompanied them to the movie and other events. Nothing like this had ever occurred at the hospital, and it was much enjoyed by the patient workers. This became a regular event every six months.

Rehab Therapy

The hospital operated an occupational therapy treatment program and had been working with select patients for almost twenty years. The area used for occupational therapy was located in a basement of one of the wards. It held rug looms, a ceramics class, an art class, and other programs where the patients received training. The occupational therapy department had a staff of about ten ladies and one supervisor.

In 1960, the hospital board decided to construct a new building that would be known as the Rehabilitation Services Building. This was the beginning of better programs, more trained staff, and some new equipment. Each department of the rehab division had supervisors, and an office for each was located in the new building.

Hundreds of patients participated in this treatment center. Each ward had a time and date for patients to attend occupational therapy, recreation therapy, industrial therapy, and sheltered workshop.

Occupational Therapy

In 1960, the occupational therapy unit moved from a basement to the new building just constructed. Mrs. Jesse was the chief of the new Occupational Therapy Building, and along with about six or eight employees, she worked daily with patients. The therapy consisted mainly of crafts, rug making, art, and ceramics.

The occupational therapy program began in the late 1940s and still continues to be one of the prime areas for a patient to have recreational and hands-on therapy. Items made by the patients were sold in the little store at the building. Patients usually received small amounts of money for their work. The balance of the sale funds were deposited in hospital trust fund accounts. Supplies and other material were purchased with these funds.

Recreation Therapy

The hospital always employed a couple of folks to operate the recreation phase of treatment in the hospital. A gym-like building was constructed in the early 1950s and was used for patient dances, basketball games, and ping-pong matches. Patients from various wards were rotated to the recreation building on a daily basis. The hospital hired a registered recreational therapist in the late '50s. Patients enjoyed this area. Prior to the construction of the All Faith's Chapel, church services were conducted each Sunday in the gym. Able patients were encouraged to attend the service of their choice. Many attended both the Protestant and Catholic services each Sunday.

The Hospital Monthly Dance

The staff and doctors chose both men and women who would be allowed to participate in the monthly hospital dance. This was a sight to see, as it was the only approved co-ed activity and the patients danced to the latest music of the time. The dances were usually attended by fifty or more patients.

Most patients did not care to participate in the dance, and the ones who did were regular attendees each month. It was remarkable that no problems ever happened during the dances, which lasted about two hours and were held during the daytime. Patients who attended thoroughly enjoyed this opportunity.

Halfway Houses

Halfway houses were new during the late '50s. Many patients who overcame most of their outward mental problems could move into one. Of course, the ward physician had to approve each transfer. Usually therapists who worked directly with the patient on a daily basis for some time could make the recommendation.

The success of the program hinged on the industrial therapist retraining the patient for a gainful task. As soon as the patient mastered the tasks, he or she was recommended for off-campus work. In the beginning, the patient would reside at the halfway house only during daylight hours. After a few weeks, if the patient responded favorably to the work environment and the new residence, he or she could start spending the night.

The ideal halfway house was supervised by an understanding individual. The patients forgot many common tasks during their confinement at the hospital. When a patient received pay for his or her work off-campus, the house custodian had to explain how to save and spend money. Most patients who were committed for several years had become accustomed to a wake-up call, a bath call, and a mealtime call and were even instructed when to change clothing. Learning to manage this on their own was a slow process and some patients failed to make this change.

I discovered that many patients were very apprehensive once nightfall came at the halfway house. Away from the hospital, sometimes it took months for patients to adjust. Sometimes the simplest tasks and decisions had to be discussed several times with them. This was the necessary retraining the patients needed to overcome their fears and desires.

It was very rewarding for a therapist to learn that patients who were kept in the hospital for many years, sometimes actually began to make the adjustment to the "outside world" and survive.

Chapter 10

Escape While I Was Assigned to Ward 12

One day, a call came in to the ward where I was working. The call stated that a mental patient had been reported wandering along Rigsby Avenue. Mr. Scott and I got in the state vehicle and proceeded to that area. As we approached the Salado Creek Bridge, we noticed a young man walking very fast toward the city.

Upon closer examination, we decided that this must be the escapee from the hospital. We quietly pulled up as close to the man as we could without causing a distraction. As we got out of the vehicle, the young man immediately ran toward the bridge and was soon under it. We ran and caught up with him but not before he disappeared into the bushes. We followed his trail to the backyard of a small home hidden in the brush. We were in for a surprise when we looked over the fence. A lion was chained to a tree behind the house.

Since the lion was chained, we decided it wasn't a threat, so we went ahead and followed the man into the small house. The escaped patient opened the door and ran into a bedroom. He jumped in the middle of the bed and started fighting and kicking us.

The residents of the home were very frightened. We later found out that they were the ones who had called the local police. We were finally able to apprehend the patient and hauled him through the brush to our vehicle. A policeman arrived just as we were putting the man in the vehicle.

The first words spoken by the patient were directed to the officer. He told the officer that he wanted to go with him and not the employees from the hospital. After a discussion with the officer, we agreed that it might be less of a threat for him to ride to the hospital in the police car. The officer handcuffed him, and we followed the police car to the Administration Building. We placed the patient in another ward that was more secure. We thanked the officer and returned to our assigned Ward 12.

Another escape incident occurred when we were escorting four patients to the clinic building for checkups and IV medications. Mr.

Scott and I were about to enter the elevator at the clinic when one of the men decided to run. We asked another employee to watch the other three so we could run after the escaped patient.

The clinic was located on the west end of the campus, close to South Presa Street. Just beyond Presa Street was the San Antonio River. This escaped patient ran directly to the river and as he jumped in, he looked back and laughed.

I am sure he thought that the two of us, all dressed in our white uniforms, would certainly not go into the river. We both paused, then jumped right in after him. We reached him just as he began to climb out on the far west bank. He was surprised that we had gone to that much effort to apprehend him. Soaking wet, all three of us returned by foot to the clinic. We took the patient directly back to the ward and released him to the attendants.

A Body Discovered at the River

One day the administration office called, and we were told that a patient was lying facedown in the river. Several staff and a couple of trustworthy patients drove in the hospital ambulance to the river. Soon we discovered the body floating in the water. Evidently, the body had been in the water for at least three or four days. We were able to pull it out with the help of several men and a hoop with a rope attached. We pulled the body to the bank nearest the ambulance. We lifted the body onto the stretcher, or gurney as some called it. Boy was the smell bad. I had never been exposed to a body that had been floating in the river for days. The stench was so bad that it made us all sick to our stomachs.

We managed to drive back to the hospital, where a local justice of the peace examined the body and ruled accidental drowning as the cause of death. We then called the contract mortician to come and retrieve it. The body was taken to the county morgue, and an autopsy was performed to confirm the cause of death. The next day, the body was taken back to the hospital for the patient workers to bury in the cemetery.

Chapter 11

Patient Stories

The Criminal Patient Who Killed a Taxi Driver in a Park in San Antonio

A notorious man about forty-five years old was committed to the hospital in the early '50s. Prior to his hospitalization, he evidently hired a taxi to take him to a local park, and while riding in the backseat, the patient pulled out a gun and shot the driver.

The shot killed the driver and the patient was sent to San Antonio State Hospital. We never knew why he was in San Antonio. He had previously been hospitalized in a New Jersey mental hospital and was released.

During my tenure on Ward 12, he was confined to an individual cell. He spent many days just dancing around the cell. He had a wicked look in his eyes. He laughed constantly about nothing. He was watched very closely and was never allowed to leave the cell. When he was fed, he would take the spoon from the tray and hold it up while dancing. Sometimes he would sing out loud or make strange noises while dancing.

One day, I had an opportunity to talk to him. I asked why he had done what he did. He told me that God sent a message to him and ordered him to kill the driver. During our conversation, all he did was laugh and speak in a tongue that was very incoherent. He never dwelled on the loss of the victim who died by his hand. After several years, the hospital legal department began making efforts to return him to his home state of New Jersey.

The patient needed to be flown to New Jersey. One of the ward doctors and I arranged the date to make the transfer. We sedated him heavily and placed a restraint around his waist and arms. While he was sedated, we dressed him with a diaper under his pants. We could not risk the chance of him leaving his seat. We then took him to the airport. We boarded the plane, pushing the patient to the door in a wheelchair. He had to be carried to his seat. We boarded prior to anyone else being seated.

The flight lasted about five or six hours, and the sedated patient didn't regain consciousness the entire trip. I suppose the passengers never knew what was going on. In the beginning of the flight, I noticed several folks staring at the patient, who was asleep, but no one asked any questions.

In New Jersey, attendants met us at the airport, and transported the patient via ambulance to a mental hospital in New Jersey. During the entire trip, the patient slept in the middle seat; the doctor and I sat on each side of him. The trip was uneventful. The main reason for transfer to New Jersey was to save the state of Texas the expense of caring for the patient. After all, New Jersey was his home state, and it was determined that he had to continue his confinement in a New Jersey hospital.

The Patient Who Loved to Injure Himself on Broken Windows

George, a fifty-year-old patient, had to be watched constantly because he had a thing for punching his fist through glass windows. There were several glass windows inside the ward. The individual cells had windows to allow daylight in, but metal grates covered the windows. The patients in the cells were not able to break the glass window because of the grating. However, on the outside of the cell, a passing patient could easily access the windows. We were fortunate that no other patient besides George desired to put their fists through them.

One day, George had appeared distressed, but no one seemed too worried about him, so he was allowed out onto the ward's grated porch. This was where the window glass in the cells was accessible. It was not unusual for patients to congregate on the grated porch, but George went out there just to admire the glass. During my two years as an intern psychiatric technician, George pushed his fist into the glass windows at least two times.

On this particular day, George waited for his opportunity to run his whole fist through the window. When he was successful, he let out a horrible scream. Upon reaching George, I noticed that his right hand was bleeding profusely. With the help of another staff member, I wrapped his arm with bandages and applied pressure since he seemed to have cut an artery close to his wrist.

We took him to the clinic as fast as we could walk, almost carrying George, who weighed at least 150 pounds. All this took place on the third floor of Ward 12. We were able to get him to the clinic, where Dr. Mac began immediately sewing up the laceration.

It was a very hot day, and the flow of blood had a smell that I was not accustomed to. We had to assist the doctor and the nurse in the treatment room. Mainly we had to restrain George to keep him from injuring the other staff and especially the elderly doctor. In about thirty minutes, George was all sewn up and ready to be taken back to his ward. I noticed that there had been no anesthetic administered before or after the surgery, but George got a big dose of penicillin before leaving.

The doctor looked at George's record and told us that this was the third time in five years that he had broken a glass window and caused deep wounds to his right arm. Several scars supported this fact.

When my assignment was finished on Ward 12, I lost contact with George, but an attendant told me that a couple of years later George had again forced his hand through another window. The attendant told me that George almost died that last time because no one noticed the incident or the injury right away.

George lay in a pool of blood with several patients standing over him, staring and saying nothing. Luckily, an attendant making his regular rounds saw George and started emergency treatment. This was one of many sad cases at the hospital. I was told many years later that they replaced the glass windows with plastic. Plastic material was unheard of at the hospital until the late '60s. George, I was told, died of a heart attack about six years after his last bout with glass windows.

Shannie

Shannie was a male patient in his late fifties. During my tenure at the hospital, he never received any real therapy or counseling. He pretty much had the run of the place and resided on an open ward. In the beginning, he refused to do any type of work, stayed by himself, and usually read books from the library. He spent a lot of time writing what looked like letters.

I visited with him one day and asked him if he would like to work in the woodworking shop. He seemed surprised and stated that he had drawn up an "invention" and would like to experiment with his design. He briefly told me that he had designed a crawling water sprinkler and had never been able to prepare a model of it. The woodworking shop fit his plans, and soon he began to work on his project. It took him at least two months of work to finally make his model.

One day, he confided in me by showing me some letters he had written to the local newspaper. I was shocked to read them, as I had been reading them in the newspaper for several years. He always signed the articles "*non-compos mentis*."

The newspaper columnist always published his works just as he wrote them and always signed them by his chosen pen name. Most of the articles were attempts to expose the hospital and the treatment of the mental patients. No one had known who had actually written the articles, which had been published for several years.

One day, Shannie evidently secured a handgun while on a visit to the city. He kept the handgun well hidden until the day he chose to use it. On the desired day at the desired time, he took his gun with him, went to the hospital superintendent's office, and asked the secretary if he could speak to the doctor. He was told that the doctor was not in the office and was away somewhere on the hospital campus.

Shannie then went to his ward doctor, entered his office, and shot him. Then Shannie turned the gun on himself. Both the doctor and Shannie died of gunshot wounds.

The hospital superintendent was lucky that day, as Shannie was probably going to kill him as well. Shannie had full off-ground privileges, which included going to town on the city bus. Patients like Shannie suffered from paranoia. This type of mental illness was the hardest to treat. Most of the paranoia patients did not have such privileges. Shannie's privileges were an exception to the rule, as he had kept his plans secret until he was ready to carry out the kill.

The Tobacco Sack Man

Freddie was a patient who was approximately sixty years old. He collected Bull Durham tobacco sacks. When he was able to collect almost two hundred tobacco sacks, Freddie patched them together and made a complete suit. He made pants and then a jacket, all out of the Bull Durham Tobacco sacks.

Freddie was the talk of the hospital. In fact, when official visitors and student nurses came to study at the hospital, Freddie wore his handmade suit. The nursing director kept the well-worn tobacco sack suit in her office for safekeeping until it was time for Freddie to put it on and display it.

Freddie was a simple type of individual who never spoke much and stayed to himself. He did, however, seem to enjoy all the attention of the visitors when he wore his tobacco sack suit. He remained in the hospital the rest of his life. Today, the whereabouts of the tobacco sack suit are unknown.

The Woman Who Drowned Her Children in a Bathtub

Hortencia was admitted to the female criminal ward by court order. She was transferred from the county jail to the hospital after psychiatric teams assured the jail authorities that Hortencia was indeed a serious mental case. Hortencia was housed in the maximum security ward at the hospital. The nurses said she had extreme nightmares and woke up screaming many nights. They sedated her well at night for several months. The staff doctors and nurses worked with her for almost six months before she was able to go outside with attendants for a walk.

Her mental state improved rapidly over the next year, and she was soon able to walk with a group to the occupational therapy clinic. At the OT she was able to work on the rug looms, which mainly exercised her body and provided therapy to her mind. She continued to take medication to assist her with her thoughts. Electroshock was also administered to her at least twice a month and then decreased to only once per month. Eventually, after two years she was able to come and go on the grounds without any problem. This type of patient remained indefinitely as a ward of the state, and I suppose she remains there to this day.

Old Jim the Carpenter

This patient was in his sixties and had been a resident of the hospital for almost thirty years. Until 1960, Jim just sat and stared at the other patients, minding his own business. He was a very likeable person who in his early years had threatened his entire family of farmers. He had become very unmanageable at home, and the family feared that Jim would hurt someone.

The county judge and county physiatrist decided to confine Jim to the state hospital. He was in his thirties when admitted. When the hospital began industrial therapy, Jim was recommended by his ward physician to begin some sort of work. Jim was accustomed to operating some woodworking machines, so with supervision he entered the industrial therapy section as a woodworker. Jim did really well and even manufactured several useful wood items that were placed for sale in the OT sales office.

The occupational therapy section operated a sales office where items were sold to staff and visitors, and a portion of the funds from the sales went into the patients' trust accounts. The trust accounts made the deposits and issued the patients coupon books that could be used in the hospital store and café.

I have to say that this was the changing element in Jim's life. He was finally able to have money (coupons) to spend as he wished. He even purchased items in the hospital store for some of his hospital friends. Jim was enjoying life for the first time after a confinement of more than thirty years, making practically no constructive accomplishments. The new industrial therapy section was a great savior for this type of long-term patient. Jim never had any visits from his family in all the years of his confinement at the hospital. He very seldom mentioned anything about his family.

The Hospital Artist

Mona, a schizophrenic patient who was about fifty years old, was a master with a paintbrush. Her product was indeed very schizophrenic; she painted dark colors and weird images. Her physician liked to examine her work and attempt to see what Mona was thinking about at the time of her painting. Mona continued to paint mostly landscapes, and usually the paintings revealed some strange thoughts. The colors she used were always dark. She often painted large eyes, sometimes even in the trees. It was depressing to examine some of her work. She hardly ever made any comments about what she was painting.

Mona was given all the paints, brushes, and canvases that she wanted. She did many paintings, and some were sold in the OT store. There was not much demand from the regular shoppers at the store; however, physiatrists who visited were interested in her paintings and her case in general. As far as I know, none of the paintings were publicly sold outside the hospital.

The Manic Cigarette Smoker

Frank, a manic-depressive patient often collected several hospital-issued packages of Bull Durham tobacco. Frank would take a newspaper, roll a giant cigarette, go to the porch, and smoke the thing. If you were able to watch this process, you would think the ward was on fire. It was just Frank smoking. He only attempted to do this when he was at the height of his manic spell. Frank also liked to stand on his head against the grate in the ward. He would stay there until a staff member forced him to stop. If not watched, he would attempt to stand on his head again. Frank caused many fights when he was in the manic mood. He was a regular recipient of electroshock. His manic period usually lasted a couple of weeks, then he would go into a stupor so deep he had to be spoon-fed. In a month or two, the manic period would resurface, and the cycle repeated. When tranquilizers were discovered, Frank began this treatment, and it mellowed him out so that he no longer did manic things.

However, Frank lived between a manic and depressive disorder most of his adult life. In later years, he did not fight any longer and remained to himself and did practically nothing but ward cleaning. He refused to enter other therapies such as OT and industrial therapy. He also did not respond to any treatment. He resembled a patient who had under gone a lobotomy. However, a lobotomy had never been preformed on him.

Big Willie

Willie weighed at least 280 pounds. He was a tall individual, about six and a half feet. He was a very simple-minded person who often cried and begged for items. Once I witnessed Willie talking really loudly and cursing at another patient. He was so big that he had no problem picking the other patient up and slamming him onto the floor. Willie did not know his strength and many times did things like picking up a heavy laundry cart and throwing it against the ward walls. Usually Willie was quiet and pretty well mannered. He did not have any friends on the ward and usually remained alone, standing next to the outside ward porch grates.

Willie was always dressed in blue overalls and heavy work shoes. He ate two trays of food in the dining hall. Willie would have a temper fit if he was not provided the extra food. Otherwise, he was no real problem unless someone teased him. He would then go into a rage and sometimes hurt the individual who had provoked him.

When tranquilizers were available to the patients, Willie became easy to control, and attendants could work with him without his tantrums. After a few months of tranquilizer treatment, Willie was able to begin working outside the ward. He usually worked on the farm detail. He had been reared on a farm in South Texas, so he understood the tasks assigned to him. Willie was later transferred to an open ward where he had freedom to come and go as he wished.

Charlie the Homosexual

Charlie was a male patient, about forty five or fifty years old. He had spent most of his life confined to Ward 12. He was a very active homosexual and confronted just about every male patient on the ward at one time or another.

He was a regular candidate for shock therapy. This therapy did not change his choice to perform sexual acts on the male patients, which was usually done at night in the male dormitory. The attendants decided to lock him in a cell at night to prevent these encounters. Many times other patients severely beat him. Placing him in confinement at night helped solve most of the problems of his confrontation with other male patients. During the day he was closely watched and kept busy doing housecleaning chores. He probably resided at the hospital the rest of his life.

The Patient Sign Painter

Nat was a short Mexican man who was about sixty years old. Nat suffered from a type of schizophrenia known as paranoid schizophrenia. He had a great talent for sign painting. When kept busy, Nat soon overcame a lot of his mental problems, or at least the problems were not quite as evident.

He was not that constructively active until the new hospital superintendent, Dr. Bennett, came on board. Dr. Bennett, being a retired military officer, had signs erected throughout the hospital. Nat was chosen to craft each one. I remember that all the signs had a silver background and bold black lettering.

Prior to Dr. Bennett's arrival at the hospital, there had been practically no visible signs naming the streets or buildings. Dr. Bennett discovered Nat and recognized his talent. Nat painted signs to mark the streets, buildings, and wards. A sign graced every doorway. All the offices soon had the doctors' names on their doors.

Once the signs were painted, the carpenter shop installed them on orders of the superintendent.

Nat was very good at freehand, especially with sign work. One day, I went to his little work area and watched him paint the lettering. I asked Nat to show me a few pointers to letter a sign. He quickly painted an *o*. While he did this, he told me to always paint the top oval and then the bottom oval and then connect the two. I was amazed; the *o* on his sign was perfect. Nat said the letter *o* was the hardest to paint correctly. I asked him to allow me to paint a few letters. I did exactly as he instructed me, and the sign I began painting turned out pretty good. Nat told me that it took many years to really be a sign painter. I remember his instructions years later when my children needed me to prepare a school poster.

Eventually, I was able to get Nat contracting signs outside the hospital for private firms and individuals. He enjoyed this off-campus work and was soon able to ride the city bus to any location. Nat, with his paints and brushes in hand, would stay gone most of the day.

Industrial therapists work with the ultimate goal of helping patients regain their composure and hopefully gain employment outside the hospital. Of all the patients I had the privilege of working with, Nat was the most successful. He was able to move into a halfway house off campus. I think this patient remained out of the hospital setting even after confinement of many years.

A New Career

In 1964, the state hired a new superintendent who had a different vision concerning the hospital. He began to put a stop to the workshop. He also decided to make a ruling that no patient would be allowed to perform a work task. This created a problem, as there were no paid employee housekeepers on the hospital staff. Janitors and housekeepers had to be hired to perform all the cleaning of the wards. My feelings were and still are that the sheltered workshop was a great improvement in the rehabilitation of the mental patients at the hospital. The new superintendent thought otherwise. After all of my efforts to continue the workshop failed, I decided it was time to find other employment.

In the summer of 1964, I was introduced to a new business selling insurance. I was appointed as an agent for a large insurance company. That became my new profession. At the time of writing this book, I have served the citizens of San Antonio, Texas, in the capacity of an insurance agent for more than fifty years. During this time, I was elected to the board of trustees at East Central School District. I remained on that board for nine years, seven of which I served as chairman. During 1987, my ninth year as trustee, I was elected as a state representative, District 119, Bexar County, Texas.

I served two terms in the Texas House of Representatives and then returned to my insurance business, where I currently remain an agent for the same company. Having a love for the mental hospital, I served on the San Antonio State Hospital Volunteer Council for several years. I was able to witness many new medical changes in the treatment of patients, all for the betterment of patient care. The sheltered workshop was closed after I left my employment at the hospital. This was a tragedy, as industrial therapy and the sheltered workshop were obviously beneficial to the patients' recovery and quality of life.

Chapter 12

Recently, the state hospital system began releasing patients by simply turning them loose. *The San Antonio Express-News* began to expose the tragedy of the hospital releasing patients by providing them only a bus ticket. These tickets were given to many patients so that they would have an opportunity to go somewhere away from the confines of the mental hospital. We do not know just how many of these former patients were given this dead-end trip.

Recently, in a front page article, *The San Antonio Express-News* claimed that at least one patient had been found dead a few days after being discharged and provided a bus ticket[3]. The Texas legislature has begun an investigation into the new method of "getting rid" of some patients. This publicity caused a disturbance among the administrative staff at the hospital and there has been no more public announcement of patients leaving via this method. One would hope a better plan was implemented than a bus ticket with nowhere to go. Most patients are not welcome in their former homes and giving them a bus ticket to their former residence has been exposed as a cruel and unusual system of discharge. Halfway houses have been able to successfully house some patients, but funds are limited. Yes, many of the patients still residing at the hospital remain castaways.

A recent article in the local newspaper, *San Antonio Express-News,* shed light on the plight of the mental health system.[4] There seemed to be a flood of mentally ill people housed in the local county jail. The hospital attempted to find ways to lower the census of the hospital. Many times, when patients are released into the community, they soon find themselves residents of the county jail. Last year the state legislature passed a law that required swift examination of folks who were mentally ill and residing as prisoners in the local jails.

---

3 Karisa King, "Patient drop-offs targeted," *San Antonio Express-News*, May 22, 2009.

4 Brian Chasnoff and Melissa Fletcher Stoeltje, "Mental health funds lag in Texas," *San Antonio Express-News*, August 7, 2010.

The reason for delays in examination and treatment of prisoners is said to be lack of funding by the state. Texas is said to rank forty-ninth of all states in mental health funding. Even then, the state is forcing cuts from the funds currently provided for the mental hospitals. This alone requires a reduction of beds. When a mentally ill person is arrested for even minor infractions of the law and is sent to jail, it causes the jail population to explode throughout the state.

> A closer look one could think it is possible that some of all inmates in jails are seriously mentally ill. In San Antonio we might find that as many as almost a third of the inmates are suffering from mental illness. I think the courts should should order exams and receive the results before proceeding with the inmate's cases.
>
> Perhaps one day the state will find funds to treat inmates with mental illness who are housed in jails and prisons throughout the state. A big problem in the jails is that there are too many mentally ill inmates and not enough qualified physicians and psychiatrists available to examine, treat, and prescribe the proper medications. Some say the waiting is weeks and even months before a mentally ill inmate is finally diagnosed and committed to the mental hospital. At the same time, the mental hospitals are overloaded and beds are not available to properly house an inmate who may have criminal charges.
>
> The following is an excerpt from an article written by Melissa Fletcher Stoeltje and published in the San Antonio Express-News on September 2, 2012 titled "Mentally Ill Receive Unequal Aid"[5]

---

5 Ibid

> "Untold number of people with mental illness live in boarding houses across the city... no one knows how many, no official registry kept....some of the homes are run by people with mental disorders"
>
> Even though Medicaid does fund some services for the mentally ill in Texas----it does not address housing. Some advocates have said that it appears housing is "ramshackle environment"
>
> "We are basically warehousing people (in boarding homes) These places are ripe for corruption, neglect and all sorts of horrible things," Stated Katrina Gay, director of communications for the National Alliance on Mental Illness.
>
> "Unfortunately, the Lone Star State doesn't fare so well in an important measure of public health.....We are last among the states in per capita spending on people with mental disabilities" said Texas Senator Carlos Uresti: South Side Reporter May 31, 2012
>
> "The lack of services and available hospital facilities is evident in our county jails; many have become default treatment centers for the mentally ill......On an average day 25 percent of the prisoners in the Harris County Jail receive psychotropic medication," said Senator Uresti.

While I spent my time ministering to the mentally ill patients, I learned that *all are human beings and created by God.* ***Even though their paths did not go in the right direction, we must remember that they are human beings and should be treated as such.***

Bibliography

The Handbook of Texas Online. "San Antonio State Hospital." Last modified on February 1, 2013. http://www.tshaonline.org/handbook/online/articles/sbs04